Life, Ritual, and Religion
Among the Lacandon Maya

The Wadsworth Modern Anthropology Library

Life, Ritual, and Religion
Among the Lacandon Maya

R. Jon McGee
Southwest Texas State University

Wadsworth Publishing Company
Belmont, California
A Division of Wadsworth, Inc.

Anthropology Editor: *Peggy Adams*
Editorial Assistant: *Karen Moore*
Production Editor: *Angela Mann*
Designer: *Donna Davis*
Print Buyer: *Barbara Britton*
Copy Editor: *Steven M. Bailey*
Compositor: *Kachina Typesetting*
Cover: *Donna Davis*
Cover Illustration: *Adriann Dinihanian*

Printed in the United States of America   49

1 2 3 4 5 6 7 8 9 10—93 92 91 90

Library of Congress Cataloging in Publication Data

McGee, R. Jon. 1955–
   Life, ritual, and religion among the Lacandon Maya / R. Jon McGee.
      p.   cm. — (Wadsworth modern anthropology library)
   Includes bibliographical references.
   ISBN 0-534-12186-1
   1. Lacandon Indians—Religion and mythology. 2. Lacandon Indians—
Rites and ceremonies. 3. Najá (Mexico)—Social life and customs.
I. Title. II. Series.
F1221.L2M4   1990
972'.004974—dc20   89–37292
                                                          CIP

ISBN 0-534-12186-1

 Contents

This book is dedicated to the people of Najá.
Without their cooperation and endless patience
my work with the Lacandon
would not have been possible.

🦋 Foreword to the Series

Modern cultural anthropology encompasses the full diversity of all humankind with a mix of methods, styles, ideas, and approaches. No longer is the subject matter of this field confined to exotic cultures, the "primitive," or small rural folk communities. Today, students are as likely to find an anthropologist at work in an urban school setting or a corporate boardroom as among a band of African hunters and gatherers. To a large degree, the currents in modern anthropology reflect changes in the world over the past century. Today there are no isolated archaic societies available for study. All the world's peoples have become enveloped in widespread regional social, political, and economic systems. The daughters and sons of yesterday's yam gardeners and reindeer hunters are operating computers, organizing marketing cooperatives, serving as delegates to parliaments, and watching television news. The lesson of cultural anthropology, and this series, is that such peoples, when transformed, are no less interesting and no less culturally different because of such dramatic changes.

Cultural anthropology's scope has grown to encompass more than simply the changes in the primitive or peasant world, its original subject matter. The methods and ideas developed for the study of small-scale societies are now creatively applied to the most complex of social and cultural systems, giving us a new and stronger understanding of the full diversity of human living. Increasingly, cultural anthropologists also work toward solving practical problems of the cultures they study, in addition to pursuing more traditional basic research endeavors.

Yet cultural anthropology's enlarged agenda has not meant abandonment of its own heritage. The ethnographic case study remains the bedrock of the cultural anthropologist's methods for gathering knowledge of the peoples of the world, although today's case study may focus on a British urban neighborhood or a new American cult as often as on efforts of a formerly isolated Pacific island people to cope with bureaucracy. Similarly, systematic comparison of the experiences and adaptations of different societies is an old approach that is increasingly applied to new issues.

The books in the Wadsworth Modern Anthropology Library reflect cultural anthropology's greater breadth of interests. They include introductory texts and supporting anthologies of readings, as well as advanced texts dealing with more specialized fields and methods of cultural anthropology.

However, the hub of the series consists of topical studies that concentrate on either a single community or a number of communities. Each of these topical studies is strongly issue-focused. As anthropology has always done, these topical studies raise far-reaching questions about the problems people confront and the variety of human experience. They do so through close face-to-face study of people in many places and settings. In these studies, the core idiom of cultural anthropology lies exposed. Cultural anthropologists still, as always, go forth among the cultures of the world and return to inform. Only where they go and what they report have changed.

James A. Clifton
Series Editor

🌺 Preface

This book examines the contemporary culture of one of the few remaining non-Christian Indian groups in Mexico, the northern Lacandon Maya of southeastern Chiapas. In particular, it focuses on the religious beliefs and practices of these people. The greater part of the research for this book was conducted in the Lacandon village of Najá, the last fully non-Christian Lacandon settlement, with brief visits made to two other principal Lacandon settlements, Mensäbäk and Lacanha Chan Sayab. I worked in Najá a total of sixteen months during the period from June 1980 to March 1982. Since then, I have traveled to Najá at least once a year, in a series of visits that lasted anywhere from a few weeks to a month.

The very heart of Lacandon religion is the *balché* ritual in which the Lacandon men brew balché, a mead-like sacred beverage and ceremonial offering, to drink and feed their gods. A descriptive analysis of the rite, its variations, and the ritual implements that are used in these rituals, fills fully one-third of this book. I have divided these topics into separate chapters, but this division is artificial and does not correspond to Lacandon "ritual reality." Ritual practices, the sacrificial symbolism of Lacandon rites, the implements, and ritual foods used in Lacandon ceremonies are all a part of a larger set of interrelated cosmological beliefs that are united in the practice of the balché ceremony. Furthermore, virtually all Lacandon rituals involve brewing and consuming balché. Thus, the balché rite is a model for Lacandon ritual action. Understanding this one rite provides deep insight into Lacandon religious beliefs in general. It is fitting, therefore, that the inspiration behind this work came as I sat with a group of Lacandon men drinking balché.

In this work, I use many examples of Lacandon mythology for two reasons, both of which underline the emic/etic distinctions that are basic to anthropological research. First, mythology is used in Lacandon society as an explanation, or rationalization, of why the world exists in its present form. Consequently, it is a reflection of the world from a Lacandon (emic) viewpoint. Second, Lacandon mythology often appears to be folk history—in other words, a reflection of actual historical events through Lacandon eyes. Thus, throughout this book, I make extensive reference to common Lacandon myths in relation to historical circumstances that may have affected the ancestors of contemporary Lacandon.

The structure of this book is relatively simple. The first four chapters provide straightforward ethnographic and historical background that is useful to understanding the Lacandon way of life. Chapter One contains brief introductory remarks on the appearance of the Lacandon, their subsistence practices, and the environmental and social contexts in which they live. In this chapter, I place an emphasis on the recent changes in settlement patterns, material technology, and the persistence of their traditional religious practices.

This book is structured around the concept that contemporary Lacandon society can be fully understood only when examined through an ethnohistorical perspective. Chapter Two provides a historical perspective on the effects of the Spanish conquest of the Maya and the implications this era has for the study of the contemporary Lacandon Maya. In contrast to the view that the Lacandon are descendants of the Maya, who built the temples at Palenque and Yaxchilan, the basic premise of this chapter is that the Lacandon originated in the Yucatán. Attempting to escape from the effects of the Spaniards' conquest of the Yucatán, the Lacandon migrated to Chiapas relatively recently, probably in the mid-seventeenth century. Because the only documentary historical sources dealing with the modern Lacandon peoples are relatively recent, and the Lacandon themselves have no written histories, this chapter examines the conditions under which the sixteenth- to nineteenth-century Lacandon must have lived, referring to their mythology and scant Spanish records.

In Chapter Three, Lacandon family structure as well as their division of labor and marriage practices (including polygyny) are outlined. Also included in this chapter is a discussion of Lacandon kinship terminology, and an analysis of kin relationships between families as reflected by residence patterns in Najá. Because Najá is a small community, it is possible to trace the social structural relationships among all households in the village.

The Lacandon are swidden horticulturalists and are masters at using the rainforest's resources without damaging their environmental surroundings. Their horticultural practices are explained in Chapter Four, together with a detailed discussion concerning the wild and cultivated plants they use for food, medicine, dyes, and the like, and the game that is hunted to supplement their diets. The chapter concludes with a discussion of the Lacandon trade in tourist items. This trade is significant because it generates a great deal of money that is used to purchase processed foods and household items; it also represents a sizable portion of a Lacandon family's annual income. Although many judge this trade to be the "commercialization" of the Lacandon, the viewpoint presented here is that the tourist trade gives these small-scale farmers subsistence flexibility in the face of environmental uncertainty and provides a valuable supplement to a household's income without detracting from traditional subsistence activities.

Beginning with Chapter Five, "Ritual Objects and Sacred Places," the book turns to Lacandon religion. The origins of contemporary Lacandon ritual behavior can be traced to the religious practices of the Prehispanic Maya. This chapter outlines the relationship between Lacandon and Prehispanic Mayan ritual implements and sacred offerings as a prelude to later chapters that discuss both the principal Lacandon rites and the symbolic sacrificial themes in Lacandon ceremonies. In the course of this chapter, inedible ritual offerings (symbolic blood and food), edible sacred foodstuffs (including symbolic representations of human flesh), ritual implements, and finally, sacred places such as the god house and cave shrines are all described.

Chapter Six is concerned with Lacandon cosmology. It is primarily a description of the Lacandon pantheon of gods and their structural and functional relationship to Prehispanic Mayan deities. This chapter also describes the Lacandones' mythological accounts of the creation of the earth and human beings.

Chapter Seven is devoted to the balché ritual because of its central importance in Lacandon Maya religion. Consumption of this sacred beverage is thought to have been common among the Prehispanic Maya, and despite centuries of prohibition by the Spaniards, ritual usage of the beverage continues. In particular, the Lacandon Maya have continued their ritual use of balché, and it remains a principal feature of their contemporary ritual behavior. This rite is a key ritual in Lacandon religion because virtually all communal ceremonies are structured around brewing and consuming the beverage. The rite can be best understood as an example of what A. F. C. Wallace characterized as a "ritual of intensification," helping to maintain and promulgate traditional lore and religious beliefs, and providing a mechanism for social control. The balché ritual is described in detail in this chapter, together with an analysis of the social structural functions of the rite.

Symbolic representations of human sacrifice and ritual cannibalism survive in a variety of Lacandon rituals described in Chapter Eight. Principally, these take the forms of foodstuffs that are symbolically transformed into human flesh, the use of *annatto* (a red vegetable dye) as a substitute for blood, and humanoid figures made from both rubber and copal incense that are ritually brought to life and then burned as sacrificial offerings to the gods. The congruence between these offerings and the Prehispanic Mayan practices of human sacrifice, ritual cannibalism, and bloodletting are outlined in this chapter, together with a description of a *Nahwah* ceremony in which several of these sacrificial symbols are displayed and used.

Lacandon rituals are not differentiated so much by the forms of ceremonial actions as they are by the personal motivations or environmental situations that necessitate the rituals. Most Lacandon rites follow the balché ritual's structure. Two very important rituals, however, do not follow this pattern: the *mek'chul,* a ceremonial initiation into adulthood, and the funeral service. The conduct of these two rites of passage are described in detail in Chapter Nine. In the first half of the chapter, the ritual process by which a child becomes an adult is examined. In the latter part, Lacandon funerary practices are described together with Lacandon beliefs about death, the soul's journey through the Underworld after death, and the afterlife.

Chapter Ten discusses the future of the Lacandon Maya. Those who have worked among the Lacandon have commonly bemoaned the imminent demise of Lacandon culture, which many believe will disappear with the death of the village elders. Often, the degradation of the Lacandones' environment by the Mexican lumber and petroleum industries is used as an analogy for this process of cultural disintegration. After almost a decade of work with the Lacandon, I no longer accept this view. What is labeled the degradation of Lacandon culture is nothing more than the natural process of acculturation and adaptation. Lacandon culture is disintegrating only in the sense that "romantic-minded" anthropologists do not like the changes they are witnessing. In this final chapter, I examine this issue of cultural change and directly address the question of whether Lacandon traditional culture will die with its elders. In contrast to prevailing opinions, I see powerful social and economic factors operating in Najá that provide incentives for younger men to maintain traditional Lacandon culture. Furthermore, evidence is presented that supports the belief that young Lacandon men have internalized much more traditional lore than their elders realize. The Lacandon have had a fairly pragmatic response to Mexican culture. As the Maya have done for a thousand years, the Lacandon assimilate the outside world to fit their own lives and to meet their own purposes. They are not helpless pawns overwhelmed by outside forces as depicted in the popular media.

A central theme in this book is the relationship among Lacandon religion, mythology, history, and the everyday lives of contemporary Lacandones. Religion is an intrinsic part of their existence. In the Lacandon world view, life is not divided into sacred and profane: Both are inextricably intertwined. The fruits of the milpa fields and the animals of the forest are the property of the gods, to give or withhold as they see fit. One who takes of these gifts must do so in a proper, moral frame of mind. The gods grant the necessities of life, such as good harvests and health, only as long as men make regular offerings of various gifts. These gifts—usually food, drink, and incense—act to reassure the Lacandon deities that they are not forgotten, thus ensuring their continued benevolence.

Just as religious beliefs and values cannot be separated from secular life in this society, Lacandon religion also cannot be studied as a phenomenon separate from the people's history and mythology. Symbolism in Lacandon ritual is deeply rooted in the ritual behavior of the Lacandones' prehispanic ancestors. In particular, the representation of human sacrifice and symbolic representations of blood are recurring themes in Lacandon rites.

Therefore, to understand contemporary Lacandon ritual, it is necessary to compare it to Prehispanic Mayan religion as it was practiced before the Spanish conquest.

Finally, before beginning, I would like to include a note on the pronunciation of Lacandon terms used in the text. I am not a linguist and have not strictly followed the phonetic alphabet in my transcription of Lacandon terms. Instead, I have adopted the system of spelling used by Robert D. Bruce (1974) in his work on Lacandon mythology. Words are pronounced in a manner similar to English but with the following exceptions (also see the Glossary):

A superscript question mark [ˀ] denotes a glottal stop that is similar to the English exclamation "oh! oh!"

An umlaut [¨] over an [a] is pronounced like the [u] in *but*.

An [x] is pronounced as [sh]. For example, the Mayan word *pixan* is pronounced as if it were written *pishan* in English.

🌀 Acknowledgments

The research on which this book is based was supported by grants from a variety of institutions. In chronological order they are: Behavioral Science Summer Research Fellowship, Rice University; Advanced Studies and Research, Rice University, Wenner Gren Foundation for Anthropological Research Grant #4195; Ora N. Arnold Research Fellowship, Rice University; Sigma Xi Continuing Research Grant; Committee for Visual Anthropology, University of Southern California; and the Office of Sponsored Projects, Southwest Texas State University.

I am deeply indebted to a number of people who aided me in my work with the Lacandon, for without their help this book would never have been written. I would first like to thank my friend and mentor Dr. Michael J. Rees who introduced me to the Lacandon and spent a semester teaching me the rudiments of their language. I also extend my sincere thanks to Professors Stephen A. Tyler and Michael M. J. Fischer of my Ph.D. committee. Part of this book is based on my doctoral thesis and their criticisms and comments have been incorporated into this work. I am also grateful to Professors Robert Taylor and James Clifton who read rough drafts of this manuscript and made suggestions that vastly improved the final draft of this book. Reviewers Thomas Weaver, University of Arizona and Allan F. Burns, University of Florida also provided helpful comments. I thank Donna Starnes in the Department of Media Services at Southwest Texas State University for applying her considerable photographic and computer skills to the preparation of the text's illustrations. I also want to acknowledge three of my students at Southwest Texas State, Clay Campbell, Kerisa McCarn, and Karla Eskew for their help with the more laborious aspects of manuscript preparation, and Mike Elkins for his expert proofreading skills. Additionally, I am grateful to the people at Wadsworth, particularly Peggy Adams and Angela Mann, for their advice, patience, and constant good humor during the production of this book. Finally, I want to thank my father Professor Reece J. McGee for his purchase of *The Epic of Man*. As a small boy this book provided my first exposure to the wonders of anthropology. Without it I might not have become an anthropologist.

❧ List of Illustrations

ꙮ List of Tables

CHAPTER ONE

An Introduction to the Lacandon Maya

LIVING IN THE LACANDON JUNGLE

The Lacandon Maya Indians live in the rainforest of southeastern Chiapas, Mexico. Numbering slightly fewer than 500 people, the majority of Lacandon live in three principal communities—Najá, Mensäbäk, and Lacanha Chan Sayab. Although grouped together under the name "Lacandon," they are actually two distinct cultural groups: the northern Lacandon, who live in Najá and Mensäbäk, and the southern Lacandon who live in Lacanha. These two groups differ in customs and speak slightly different dialects of the Yucatecan Maya language.

The Indians themselves are pointedly aware of these differences. All Lacandon men let their hair grow long, falling past their shoulders, but Northerners distinguish themselves from Southerners by cutting bangs across their foreheads. Southern Lacandon women leave their hair free, while northern women tie it back into a single braid, with decorations of feathers or ribbons. Both sexes wear a long white robe called a *xikul,* although women also wear skirts beneath their robes. Because the southern Lacandon wear *xikuls* that are longer than those worn in the north, the northern Lacandon call the southern group *Chukuch Nok* ("long tunics") and have traditionally avoided them because of the southerners' reputation for violence. In fact, during the period 1870–1940, homicide was a frequent cause of death among the southern Lacandon, with 74 percent of these murders the result of intragroup feuding over women (Nations 1979:135). Although a murder has not occurred since 1952, the northern Lacandons' fear of the southern group persists, and intermarriage between the two is not common even today.

The research described here was undertaken in the period between May 1980 and August 1985 among the northern Lacandon, primarily in the village of Najá, which lies approximately 65 miles south of the city of Palenque and on the shore of Lake Najá (see Figures 1.1 and 1.2). The community lies in mountainous terrain, heavily forested with pine, mahogany, ceiba, and palm trees. This area is approximately 3,000 feet above sea level and receives from 70 to 100 inches of rain each year, the heaviest

FIGURE 1.1 *Map of Mexico and the United States*

rains falling between August and November. A typical day during the rainy season begins sunny and warm with heavy showers falling by mid-afternoon. The rains usually abate by dark, and evenings are clear and cool.

The primary means of subsistence in the Lacandon jungle is swidden, or slash-and-burn agriculture. The fields *(milpas)* are usually cleared of brush and small trees in March and April. This growth is dried and burned in late April or early May in preparation for planting, which occurs just before the rains begin in June. (For a detailed look at this process, see my film "Swidden Agriculture Among the Lacandon Maya" [1986] which documents this process—see Appendix B.) The principal crops are maize and black beans, but chilis, tomatoes, squash, onions, bananas, and tobacco are also cultivated. Groves of orange, grapefruit, and tangerine trees grow near the village, and small game supplements the Lacandon diet. The common game animals found today are spider and howler monkeys, aguti, armadillo, white-tailed deer, and paca. Fish, crayfish, and snails are found in the nearby lakes, and chickens are raised for both eggs and meat.

The traditional Lacandon dwelling, as with that of most Mayan Indians, is a one-room, dirt-floored, thatch-roofed hut. Because the roof thatching extended down the side of the structure close to the ground, these houses did not have walls. Now, because the Lacandon are relatively affluent

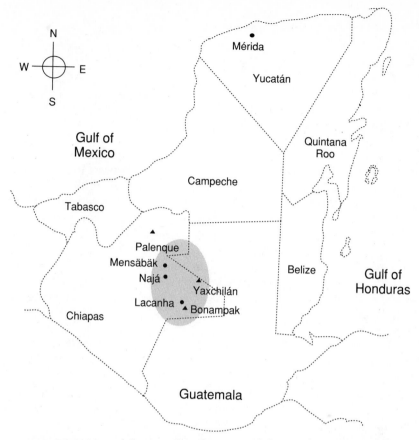

FIGURE 1.2 *Map of the Yucatán, Chiapas, and the Lacandon Jungle*

through the sale of crafts to tourists and lumbering rights to their land, the house building style also has changed. Today, the typical Lacandon house has two rooms (living room and sleeping area), a cement slab floor, board walls, and sheet tin roof. As in the past, cooking is done in a kitchen hut separate from the main house.

RECENT ENVIRONMENTAL AND SOCIAL CHANGE

Until the end of the nineteenth century, the jungle provided the Lacandon with a relatively safe refuge against unwanted contact with outsiders. By the turn of the century, however, this area became a center for commerical lumbering and the focus of immigration for Tzeltal- and Tzotzil-speaking Mayan Indians from the highlands of Chiapas. A round of epidemic diseases, introduced by lumber company workers, severely reduced the Lacandon population of this time, and the influx of thousands of Indians to the area forced the Lacandon to abandon their traditional areas of settlement for more isolated parts of the jungle. Within the first two decades of the twentieth century, the Lacandon population declined to fewer than 100 individuals, and until the 1930s, lumbermen and *chicleros* (men who tap the gum of the chicle tree, which is used in the manufacture of chewing gum) remained the Lacandon's principal source of contact with the outside world. In fact, *monterías,* or lumber camps, were an important source of trade goods for Lacandon families; here they exchanged meat, tobacco, and bows and arrows for metal tools and manufactured cloth.

The Lacandon remained relatively isolated from the outside world until after World War II, at which point Mexican industries began to exploit their jungle habitat. Most recently, this has included exploration for petroleum. Since that time, changes have come quite rapidly to the Lacandon Jungle. Probably the most significant event occurred in the summer of 1979 when a road bulldozed into the jungle by industries interested in the area's timber resources reached Najá. The village was thus connected to major cities in the area such as San Cristobal and Palenque. Before 1979, the only way to reach Najá was by airplane, mule, or foot. Although travel is still often not easy, the automobile is now a common means of transportation. Today, the people of Najá own three trucks, as does the community of Mensäbäk. In the dry season when the road is passable, these Lacandon villages are only a few hours from the cities of Palenque, Tenosique, Emiliano Zapata, Ocosingo, and San Cristobal, all formerly at least two or three days' journey by foot. Yet, even with these changes, the most reliable means of travel remains walking, for the long rainy season often makes the road impassable and travel by air precarious. For example, in October 1981, flooding washed out two of the bridges on the road between Najá and Palenque, severely restricting travel by truck.

In 1940, the Mexican government's agrarian reform laws were applied to eastern Chiapas so that much of the rainforest was declared national territory and opened to colonization. This encouraged an influx of immigrants into the Lacandon Jungle, mostly Tzeltal and Chol Maya. These Indians are the descendants of the area's original inhabitants, who were captured, converted, and resettled into mission towns such as Ocosingo by Spanish colonial administrators in the sixteenth and seventeenth centuries. The flow of people into the jungle continues today as Tzotzil and Tzeltal Maya continue to leave the highlands of Chiapas for unoccupied lands in the Lacandon Jungle.

Unfortunately, this migration of Indians has had a severe environmental influence on the Lacandon and their environment. Cattle and pig husbandry were brought to the jungle by these new settlers. In order to obtain forage for their livestock, the newcomers seeded abandoned milpas with grasses instead of allowing them to lie fallow and regenerate their soil nutrients and natural plant growth. Land treated in this manner soon becomes useless for agriculture unless it can be worked with intensive agricultural techniques (such as plowing) that are not available to the Indians. In this fashion, not only has the jungle been rapidly shrinking in size but also erosion quickly ravages the land as tree cover is cut.

Another consequence of this process is that the number of game animals in the forest has been drastically reduced as the ranges of these animals are destroyed. Paradoxically, when the new immigrants attempted to increase their food production by raising livestock, they decreased available food resources represented by traditional game animals of the forest. Twenty years ago, the forests were filled with deer and monkey, and Lacandon men tell stories of hearing jaguars prowling in the night. Now, game is increasingly rare. Consequently, traditional Lacandon patterns of production, resource utilization, and nutrition have all been altered in the last few decades. For example, as game resources decreased, the Lacandon developed an increasing reliance on manufactured foods such as canned meats. Unlike game killed in a hunt, these processed foods must be bought. Thus, Lacandon men now spend time constructing crafts that can be sold to tourists, instead of working in their milpas or hunting.

In self-defense, the Lacandon sought legal ownership of the lands on which they live, and in 1971, the Mexican government declared 614,321 hectares of Chiapan rainforest a national park with the Lacandon its only legal residents. But this grant of land included only the community of Lacanha Chan Sayab, and not until 1975 was the park area expanded to 662,000 hectares in order to incorporate the villages of Najá and Mensäbäk. Although the park was created in an attempt to protect the Lacandon, little effort has been expended to enforce the park's boundaries. As a result, thousands of Indians from other parts of Mexico continue to move into this land and push the Lacandon out. This process is dramatically illustrated each time I drive into Najá. Every year more jungle is cut. Ten years ago, within an hour of leaving Palenque one would be in primary forest. Today, it takes several hours to once again reach the forest. Even more ominous is that each time I return there is more barbed wire fencing off land that is supposedly a national reserve created to protect the Lacandons' traditional lifestyle.

One obvious result of the increasing population pressure in the Lacandon Jungle has been a fundamental alteration in the traditional settlement pattern of Lacandon families. Formerly, the Lacandon lived in isolated family compounds hidden in the middle of their milpas, separated even from friends and relatives by miles of jungle. They preferred to avoid strangers and only rarely visited other Lacandon families. Today, the Lacandon live in villages as a form of self-protection against the invasion of outsiders who steal from their milpas, destroy the forest with improper swidden techniques, and drive away game animals.

Visitors to the Lacandon Jungle often arrive expecting to see either savages or Mayan flower children in harmonious communion with their jungle environment, and I am often asked whether the Lacandon use mushrooms or marijuana to get high. (No. They are unequivocally against the use of both substances.) These people are disappointed by the fact that the Lacandon have readily adapted to technological change, and enjoy gadgets just as does any suburban American. As early as the eighteenth century, the Lacandon exchanged tobacco and bows and arrows for metal tools, although the use of steel machetes and axes probably did not become common until the turn of this century. By the 1940s, the bow and arrow, although still in use, was being rapidly replaced by the rifle. Metal grinders have replaced manos and metates except when ceremonial food-stuffs are prepared, and manufactured cloth is now used instead of hand-woven cotton cloth. Flashlights, radios, cassette-tape players, matches, rubber boots, and rifles are all common household items today, replacing traditional pieces of equipment.

Social changes also have occurred among the Lacandon, one of the biggest areas of change being religion. In the mid-1950s, a Maya-speaking American Baptist missionary succeeded in convincing the southern Lacandon of Lacanha Chan Sayab to abandon their traditional gods and rituals and convert to Protestant Christianity. As a part of this conversion process, traditional dress (the xikul) and appearance (shoulder-length uncut hair) have been abandoned by the southern Lacandon.

By 1973, a Yucatecan Maya–speaking missionary for the Seventh Day Adventist Church succeeded in eradicating any expression of traditional Lacandon belief (including music and songs) among the people of Mensä-bäk. Today, an impressive cement block temple sits on a hill overlooking the village (Figure 1.3), and members of the community follow dietary restrictions set down in the Old Testament book of Leviticus. Robert Bruce, who was present during the conversion process, describes several of the changes imposed on the people of Mensäbäk:

> The first of numerous restrictions was the declaration that approximate-ly half of the Lacandones' traditional game and fish were unkosher. Liquor, beer, and the ceremonial drink called *balché* or anything else alcoholic, together with tobacco in any form were sinful. The polygamous households were broken up. A man could keep only his first wife. The others though they may have been happily married for ten or twenty years, discovered that they had been living in sin; each was obliged to leave the husband and marry some bachelor [with the result that several young men have old women for wives—RJM] (Bruce and Perera 1982:21–22).

The northern Lacandon of Najá have proven to be more resistant to change. They have actively discouraged missionary activity in their village since the 1940s, choosing to retain their traditional gods and modes of worship. Some men from Najá go so far as to characterize the words of the missionaries as *wolol tus,* or "all lies." The families in Najá also have altered the traditional pattern of postmarital residence in the marriages of their daughters as a means of preserving their families' traditional religious orientation. Formerly, after completing his bride service, a Lacan-don husband would take his wife and create his own independent family household. Today, a young man who marries a woman from Najá usually remains with her in the village, building a house near his father-in-law's

FIGURE 1.3 *Seventh Day Adventist temple in Mensäbäk*

household. In effect, a man who marries into a family in Najá also makes a commitment to retain his affiliation with traditional Lacandon rituals.

The people of Najá have managed to maintain their traditional belief system, while virtually every other Maya Indian group in Mexico has adopted some aspects of Christianity and become acculturated into mainstream Mexican society. As a consequence of this self-enforced isolation, the Lacandon of Najá possess a traditional religious/ritual system uninfluenced by Mexican cultural contact. This makes the people of Najá ethnologically important, for the main source of ethnographic information on Precolumbian Mayan civilization are accounts by Spanish priests, soldiers, or Indians educated in Spanish schools. The opportunity to study a Mayan belief system untainted by Spanish or Christian thought is extremely valuable, because traditional Mayan belief systems were largely forgotten or altered by the early seventeenth century as a consequence of the Spaniards' conquest of Mexico. Thus, the Lacandon are a unique window to what peasant life and religious beliefs among the ancient Maya *may* have been like. To be sure, glimpses of the past exist among other Mayan societies as well. A version of the ancient Maya divinatory calendar (the *Tzolkin*) is still utilized in the highlands of Guatemala (Tedlock 1985), and balché is still made in the Yucatán (in fact, a colleague of mine attended a balché ceremony dedicated to the Chacs, at the cenote in the ruins of Mayapan in the summer of 1980). But of all the Mayan peoples, only among the Lacandon has a coherent system of Mayan religion survived intact without influence from either Catholic or Protestant Christian belief.

Lacandon rituals are centered around the ceremonial offering of the sacred beverage balché which men brew to drink and feed their gods. A type of mead, balché is made with water, honey, and the bark of the balché tree. The mix is left to ferment for a day or two and then consumed in a rite in which the participants become moderately intoxicated. Contrary to drunkenness in our own society, intoxication on balché is thought to confer a special level of ritual purity that is necessary to interact with the deities. In fact, Lacandon men use inebriation to achieve a transcendental state of mind that they believe allows them to communicate with their gods.

The Lacandon believe their lives are a copy, or model of the lives of their deities. Just as men get drunk on balché, so too the gods enjoy the ritual beverage. Lacandon deities are believed to eat tortillas and beans as do the Indians and to live in thatched roof huts like those still used by more traditional Lacandon families. The *yatoch k'uh* ("god houses"), which are built for the storage of ceremonial implements and as a place to conduct rituals, imitate the gods' homes, and Lacandon mythology instructs as to how this "home" should be decorated with symbolic blood.

The understanding that contemporary Lacandon beliefs reflect prehispanic patterns of behavior came to me in a moment of inspiration while I participated in a Lacandon balché ceremony. In this rite, the assembled adult men spend the day drinking and offering balché to their gods. We have all experienced this feeling of sudden insight, when a problem suddenly becomes clear and we want to run naked through the streets shouting "eureka" as did Archimedes. In this instance, I had to scribble down as many ideas as possible between the continual consumption of gourds of balché being passed my way. Somehow, it seems fitting that the inspiration behind this work came as I sat with a group of Lacandon men drinking balché.

In the last forty years, this traditional belief system of the people living in Najá has successfully resisted the intrusions of Catholic missionaries and, more recently, two different forms of evangelical Protestant Christianity, while other Lacandon communities have undergone conversion and abandoned their traditional forms of worship. Yet the people of Najá are not the "last of the ancient Maya" or a people "uncontaminated" by contact with Hispanic culture. Some writers romantically imagine the Lacandon to be a version of Rousseau's noble savages, hiding from civilization in the Lacandon Jungle. I confess a fondness for this image myself, but it does not fit the reality of Lacandon life. In fact, the Lacandon are quite open to certain kinds of change, particularly technological innovations that make their lives more pleasant—such as a community truck, portable tape-cassette players, and cement floors for their houses. As much as visitors may fondly remember the good old days when the Lacandon lived in dirt-floored, thatched roof houses, I, for one, thank their gods for the introduction of cement floors, because they help to keep the flea population at tolerable levels. Still, despite these changes, many of the old beliefs are preserved. A student of the Lacandon simply has to look beyond the manufactured cloth and cassette players to find ancient facets of Prehispanic Mayan life in practice.

Working with the Lacandon

I have now provided a variety of introductory facts about the Lacandon and their lifestyle. But this information does not give a clear picture of the Lacandon as human beings, how I got along with them, or what it is like to live in a Lacandon village. These, too, are important aspects of anthropological research yet few anthropologists deal with these issues. It may be that anthropologists ignore these aspects of their work because it is difficult to write about an endeavor that is both scientific and emotionally powerful, so as scientists we concentrate on repeating ethnographic facts. Some anthropologists also are embarrassed to admit fears and mistakes in the field. I certainly goofed a few times.

I am often asked what the Lacandon think of me. This is a difficult question. Some people in Najá like me, enjoy my visits, and are sad to see me leave. Others do not care whether I am around or not. All in all, they tolerate my presence with good humor. It would be colorful to say that I was "adopted into the tribe," but I don't feel my presence or absence is of much significance to the majority of Lacandon. For that matter, the rest of the world's existence does not seem to be of great significance to the average Lacandon. If we all disappeared tomorrow, their lives would continue relatively unchanged.

The Lacandon divide humanity into three groups, *Hach Winik,* or "real people"—that is, Lacandon Maya; *Kah,* a derogatory term for other Indians; and *Tsul,* light-skinned foreigners. One's degree of humanity depends on whether you speak *hach t'an* ("real language")—that is, Lacandon Maya. Because I speak Lacandon, I am almost civilized in their eyes, although not really an adult because I do not work a milpa (garden) as do adult Lacandon men. Even though I described myself as a teacher, many men did not understand how a real adult could make a living by reading and writing. As for the rest of humanity, they speak *putun t'an* ("barbarous") or ("unintelligible language") and are thus not fully civilized. If you walked into a Lacandon village without knowing Maya, you would be an object of curiosity, but largely ignored. After all, in their eyes, you don't speak the tongue of civilized humans. Despite this attitude toward outsiders, the Lacandon are a warm and funny people. As with other Mayan peoples in my experience, the key is speaking Maya. If you speak "real language," you are admitted into a new and wholly different world from that experienced by an outsider, even one who speaks Spanish. If you behave in a proper Lacandon manner, they are a gracious people.

When I lived in Najá, I assumed the role of postadolescent "stepson" to Chan K'in Viejo, the community's ritual leader. I say "postadolescent" because I was not married and the father of children, which is characteristic of adulthood in Lacandon eyes. I was housed in a dirt-floored, thatch-roof hut in which Chan K'in Viejo's adolescent sons slept. I worked, ate, worshipped, and mourned deaths with this family. In addition to gathering my own data on Lacandon religion, I did the same tasks as Chan K'in Viejo's sons, working in his milpa, chopping wood for kitchen fires, and collecting incense to burn in his incense burners. To reduce the burden I placed on the family's resources, I also purchased supplementary food for the family such as rice, beans, canned tuna, and oatmeal.

My first introduction to the Lacandon, in the summer of 1980, was less than the exotic experience of which I had dreamed. I traveled with a friend who had worked with the Lacandon a decade earlier, and was returning to the field to continue his research. We hired a small plane in the town of Emiliano Zapata, and took off for the community of Lacanha. I had no idea what to expect but was excited by the prospects of high adventure in exotic places. Excitement soon turned to nausea as the plane bounced along through the air. Nothing dims one's sense of adventure quicker than airsickness, and my dominant memory of the flight is of fighting to keep from throwing up in the back seat of the plane.

Finally, the moment arrived. We buzzed the village and landed on a grass airstrip at the edge of the community. With great relief, I jumped from the plane into the middle of a group of men with black shoulder-length hair and wearing what looked like long, white painter's smocks. I stared at them, they stared at me, and it suddenly occurred to me that even if I had known what to say at this great moment I had no idea how to say it. My friend immediately greeted these men and walked off in animated conversation with a group of his old friends, leaving me standing alone with our equipment encircled by a group of Lacandon who began looking through our baggage. One man asked me a question in Lacandon, and I could do nothing but stand there with a foolish look on my face, saying "no entiendo," which is Spanish for "I do not understand." I have never felt so conspicuous or intimidated in my life.

Because I could not communicate with adults, I spent the next several weeks following Lacandon children around, building my vocabulary by asking them the names of things. The first Lacandon phrase I learned was *bainke lati?,* or "What is this?" Because I was a novelty in the village and possessed lots of things they could play with, the children were good-natured about my ignorance, and with their help I mastered a rudimentary Lacandon vocabulary by the end of the summer.

It is difficult to describe how it feels to live in a Lacandon village. By American standards the pace of life is slow. The Lacandon have no holidays or weekends, thus each day blends with the previous day in a never-ending cycle that is organized around the production of food. The features that mark the passing of time are not birthdays or holidays; the Lacandon do not use a calendar for marking those events. Instead, the growing cycle of crops in the milpa, onset of the summer rains, cooling of the weather, or cycles of the moon are the significant events in Lacandon time.

The Lacandon have no television, movies, or books. There are no restaurants, shopping malls, or video stores. Instead, conversation is an art form in Lacandon families. People sit by their fires at night, listening to the elders tell stories about ancient times, discussing the day's events, or listening to music on their radios. Although they do not have the diversions found in western society, the Lacandon have a strong sense of communal identity that I do not see in American society. Americans view themselves as individuals, and we guard our privacy with walls, fences, dark sunglasses, and stereo headphones. On the other hand, there is little privacy in a Lacandon village because they perceive themselves not so much as individuals, but as parts of a larger, extended family group. In their eyes, one who wants privacy must be up to no good. On a personal level, this attitude meant that many of my actions were not solitary activities. In particular, bathing was a spectator sport. I would usually go to the men's bathing area accompanied by a group of young boys who would want to sample my shampoo, play with my shaving cream, and comment on the hairiness of my body in comparison to theirs. Shaving in particular, was a source of continual amusement to them. This lack of privacy was one of the more difficult aspects of life in Najá. One of my favorite retreats was to retire to my hammock at night, take out my shortwave radio, and listen to the Armed Forces Radio broadcasts of Monday Night Football. It was one activity I could do alone because no one else understood the English language broadcast and I couldn't explain the rules of football in Lacandon.

This extended sense of family membership also results in a larger degree of sharing than in American society. In many respects, personal property is family property in Lacandon society, and I quickly found that if I wanted to be treated as a member of a Lacandon family I had to act as one, which meant discarding the notion that possessions I brought with me to Najá were strictly mine. To avoid accusations of stinginess, most of my equipment to some degree became communal property of the family I lived with. Buying a special treat such as chocolate meant having one bite and then sharing the rest among twenty expectant people.

What is it like to live in Najá? At one time or another, it has been mentally demanding and boring. Other times were exhilarating, lonely, and sometimes sad. When I think about living in Najá, I usually remember two very different experiences, one negative, the other positive.

One of my worst experiences in Najá was lying in my hammock late one night listening to a group of men in a neighboring house argue about whether I should be allowed to continue my stay in the community. Earlier that day, I had gotten into a public argument about the use of one of the community's trucks. This argument precipitated the late-night discussion of my future in Najá.

Only two men in the village know how to drive. Because a member of the family I was living with was seriously ill, I asked to borrow a truck to drive to Palenque and buy medicine. I was told I could hire one of the two men to drive me, but I could not borrow a truck. The argument escalated when I protested this decision, saying I should not have to pay in order that I might buy medicine for a member of the community. He retaliated with a list of accusations concerning how foreigners came to Najá to steal from the Lacandon and how I had no business being there. The argument attracted a crowd of spectators who watched in complete silence. Angry, frustrated, and realizing there was no way to win this argument, I finally walked away, leaving my antagonist lecturing those watching about how I should be required to leave the village. That night, I lay in the dark in my hammock, angry and miserable, listening to the debate about my future, unable to speak on my own behalf. I am happy to say that calmer individuals prevailed at the meeting, and I was allowed to continue my work in Najá.

On the other hand, one of my favorite experiences in Najá was sitting on the doorstep of my hut and watching the sun set over the mountains to the west. No matter what had happened that day, I always found it soothing to watch the sun set surrounded by the sensations of evening descending upon the village. In particular, I think of the household sounds and smells such as corn being ground for the evening's tortillas, women conversing in quiet voices as they worked, and the smell of food cooking over the open hearths.

I am often asked what I missed most while living in Najá. My answer, without hesitation, is hot water for bathing. This excerpt from my field diary will give you an indication of why I feel this way.

January, 1982

I have not written much in the last couple of days and have forgotten what day it is. I am in a rotten mood and do not feel like speaking with anyone this afternoon. It is cold and I stink. This is the third day straight of constant rain and it is too cold to bathe. I keep hoping the clouds will break and the sun will come out long enough for me to get a bath but so far no luck. Bathing in the stream is cold even on warm sunny days, on a day like this it would be freezing. The main question occupying my mind today is how filthy can I get before I can't stand it any longer. I think I would hitch a ride to Palenque just for a hot shower in my current state of mind.

Along with bathing, I wish the sun would come out so that things would dry out a little bit. Everything is damp—clothes, sleeping bag, duffle bag, notebooks—and smells like mildew. I have been soaked to the skin at least once a day for the past week but there hasn't been enough sun to get things fully dried out. I have my camera, tape recorder, and notebooks wrapped in plastic bags so nothing has gotten directly wet, but the dampness is taking its toll. I wish I had some safe and dry place where I could store my notebooks and clean up the equipment. Everything has built up a nice layer of grime. I am being called for lunch. I'll finish this later.

Back from lunch where I noticed that nobody else in the family seems to be as wet or dirty as I am. How the hell do they do it? Maybe someone here has secretly installed a shower and clothes dryer and they are keeping it a secret from me! I wonder if they think I smell as bad as I think I smell? I have about reached the point where I am willing to risk hypothermia to be clean. I would kill for hot water right now.

Despite the lack of shower facilities, my time in Najá has been a very rewarding experience. I am always anxious to return.

In the following chapter, a historical look at the Spaniards' conquest of the Yucatán and the impact of these events on the Lacandon in Chiapas will prove an instructive preview to the study of Lacandon society as it exists today.

CHAPTER TWO

🌿 The Conquest of the Yucatán and Origins of the Lacandon

RELIGIOUS CONQUEST OF THE YUCATÁN

On March 1, 1517, a Spanish slaving expedition sailing from Cuba under the command of Francisco Hernández de Córdoba inadvertently became the first military expedition to land and fight an engagement in Mexico. Landing to replenish their water supply near a town called Potonchán (near the present day city of Campeche in the Yucatán Peninsula), the expeditioners were attacked by a large party of Mayan warriors who forced the Spanish to retreat to their ships with heavy losses. Córdoba, who died of wounds suffered in this battle, lived long enough to carry an account of his adventures back to Cuba, and in 1519, Hernando Cortez, accompanied by Francisco de Montejo (the eventual conqueror of the Yucatán) and a small military force, sailed from Cuba to the Yucatán. As Landa wrote, "When he heard the news of so much land and riches he felt a desire to see them and even to acquire them for God and his king, as well as for himself and his friends" (Tozzer, 1978:13).

Cortez, however, was unable to establish a foothold in the Yucatán and instead moved north, eventually conquering the Aztec in central Mexico. In 1526, Montejo, inspired by the success Cortez had enjoyed in central Mexico, again attempted to establish a permanent military presence in the Yucatán but was driven out in 1535. In 1540, however, Montejo and his son succeeded in conquering the southwest section of the Yucatán Peninsula in what is now the state of Campeche. From that point, with the help of Mayan allies, the conquest of the Yucatán proceeded rapidly. In 1542, the city of Mérida was founded on the site of the Indian city of Tiho in the northwest; and in 1543, the city of Valladolid was established in the northeast section of the peninsula. Missionary programs quickly followed the military's subjugation of the Yucatán. In 1544, eight Franciscan friars, four from Mexico City and four from Guatemala (conquered in 1524 by Cortez's lieutenant Alvarado), arrived in the Yucatán and founded monastic houses, each with a school and clinic, in Mérida and Campeche (Scholes and Roys 1938:585–586). By the 1560s, bishops had been appointed for both the provinces of Yucatán and Chiapas, and a program for the resettlement and conversion of the Chol-speaking Indians in Chiapas was underway. At this time, with large areas of Chiapas depopulated by resettlement and disease, Yucatecan-speaking Indians began to move south into Chiapas from the Yucatán. Thus, it was probably in the period between 1560 and 1600 that the Lacandon established themselves in Chiapas.

What were the factors in the Yucatán that could have precipitated such large-scale emigration from that area? Although some of the Spaniards undoubtedly believed in their mission to bring the word of God and civilization to the Indians, the conquest brought terrible hardships to the Mayan people. Not only warfare but also disease, slavery, and resettlement took a deadly toll on the native population. For example, concerning pacification of the Indians, Fr. Diego De Landa, appointed Bishop of Yucatán in 1572, wrote:

> The Indians of the provinces of Cochua and Chetumal revolted, the Spanish pacified them in such a way, that these provinces which were formerly the thickest settled and the most populous, remained the most desolate of all the country; committing upon them unheard of cruelties, cutting off their noses, arms, and legs, and the breasts of women, throwing them into deep lagoons with gourds tied to their feet; stabbing the little children because they did not walk as fast as their mothers; and if those they drove along, chained together around the neck, fell sick or did not move along as fast as the others, they cut their heads between the others, so as not to stop and untie them. With like inhuman treatment as this did they drag along in their train for their services a large number of male and female captives (Tozzer 1978:60–61).

The Spanish excused this type of conduct by saying that they themselves were few in number and thus could not subjugate so many people without instilling terror in them. The Spanish government also granted Montejo the right to enslave natives if they were rebellious, refused to accept Spanish domination, or rejected Christianity.

The task of converting the Indians to Christianity was implemented rapidly. Because there were few missionaries to carry out their program (no more than 380 by the late 1550s), they worked within what has been called "a context of coercion" (Clendinnen 1987:47). Indian children were given daily religious instruction, and adults were forced to attend weekly meetings. Indian lords were involuntarily baptized, and their children were taken to monastery schools for Christian instruction.

The missionaries also commonly resettled Indians into mission communities where they could be closely supervised, a program that brought great hardship to the Indians. Dispersed local populations were concentrated in areas convenient for the friars. Often without warning, Indians were ordered from their homes and herded to the new communities while their old villages were burned. Consequently, many died from hunger and exposure. Concerning these resettlement programs, the author of the *Relacion of Dzonot* wrote:

> These old Indians also say that one important reason why so many people have died was the depopulation of the pueblos where they were settled on their old sites in order to bring them near to the monasteries. . . . And in the pueblos which did not wish to leave their sites, he ordered their houses to be set on fire (Tozzer 1978:72).

A further blow to the Yucatecan Maya was the zeal with which the principles of Christianity were enforced by the Franciscan missionaries. Because there were few priests, Christian instruction of the Indians was often perfunctory and mass baptisms of hundreds of individuals at a time were common. Clendinnen (1987:49), for example, cites one Franciscan's description of a brother's feat in which between 4,000 and 6,000 Indians were baptized in one day. Given the paucity of missionaries, the circumstances under which Christian instruction was provided, and the resentment of the Maya, it is not surprising that pagan religious beliefs continued to flourish, although out of sight of the Spanish overseers. When, in the summer of 1562, it was discovered that the worship of traditional Mayan deities was still occurring (some rituals even being held in churches), Fr. Diego de Landa, then *provincial* of the Franciscan Order, began an inquisition in the province of Mani that soon spread to the neighboring provinces of Sotuta and Hocaba Homun. Convinced that idolatry was widespread, the friars had hundreds of Indians in each province arrested, questioned, then tortured to obtain confessions. According to Scholes and Roys (1938:596):

> The method [of torture] frequently employed was to suspend the Indians in mid-air by a rope tied to their waists. If this proved ineffective, heavy stones were then tied to their feet. They were also whipped while in this position, and often hot wax was dripped on their naked bodies.

The results of this inquisition, established by an official inquiry conducted in 1565, found that 157 Indians died during torture and 32 were permanently crippled. Some 4,549 men and women had been put to torture. Another 6,330 Indians who had voluntarily confessed received punishments such as fines, whipping, and periods of forced labor. Not surprisingly, as a consequence of these actions, Indian hostility and resentment toward the Spanish reached a peak at this time.

Disease also took a terrible toll on the Indian population. Diseases such as measles and smallpox that were common in Europe proved devastating to the Indian populations, who had never before been exposed to them. One study estimated that a 75 percent decline in the native population of central Mexico occurred between the years 1520 and 1600 (Borah and Cooke 1963). This mortality rate was duplicated in the Yucatán, particularly from smallpox, which was introduced by 1520. Native sources place its appearance in Katun 2 Ahau, running from June 1500 to February 1520 (Thompson 1972:52). The Spanish author of the *Relacion de Yucatán* estimated in 1579 that 90 percent of the Indian population had died in the 30 years between the conquest and 1579 because of

> . . . the great infirmities and pestilences which there have been through-out the Indies and especially in this province, namely measles, small-pox, catarrhs, coughs, nasal catarrhs, haemorrhages, bloody stools, and high fevers which customarily break out in this province (Thompson 1972:53).

At this same time, yellow fever also reached epidemic proportions; the presence of the disease is documented in the Chilam Balam of Chumayel, a book of Mayan history and prophecy. The first yellow fever epidemic in the Yucatán spread from Campeche to Mérida. From revised Spanish tribute lists, Scholes and Roys (1968:304) calculated that half the Indian population of the towns in the area died. For example, working with the records of the town of Chanaca, in the northeastern corner of the Yucatán, Scholes and Roys (1968:324) estimated that in 1528 the town had 3,000 men alone, not counting women and children. In 1543, this number had been reduced to between 600 and 700 people total; by 1579, only 20 families lived in the town. This, then, was the situation confronting the Yucatecan Maya of the mid-sixteenth century. Faced with enslavement, the inquisition, forced resettlement, and epidemic diseases, large numbers of Indians fled from the Yucatán.

ORIGINS OF THE LACANDON

What does the plight of the Yucatecan Maya have to do with the Lacandon? What I call the "immigration hypothesis" has been advanced elsewhere, but briefly stated, it suggests that the Lacandon were not the original inhabitants of the area in which they now live but are, historically speak-ing, fairly recent immigrants to Chiapas from the Yucatán peninsula. This is not a new hypothesis. It was first advanced by Tozzer at the turn of the century (1907:12) and argued ably by Scholes and Roys (1968). Here, I would like to advance this point of view one step further by examining linguistic, historical, and mythological evidence.

It is useful to begin with an analysis of the term *Lacandon* itself, for the word's historical usage by the Spanish confounds the identification of specific Indian groups in Chiapas. In the sixteenth century, the word *Lacandon* was not the name for a specific group of people as it is today. Instead, the Spanish used the term to refer to non-Christian Indians within a geographical area covering Chiapas and a part of the modern state of Tabasco. Thus, it is impossible to know exactly how many groups were lumped under the term *Lacandon,* a fact that confuses historical records considerably. As the original Lacandon were apparently a Chol-speaking people, how did this name come to refer to a small group of Yucatecan-speaking individuals? Nations (1979) believes the Lacandon came to Chiapas from the Yucatán via Guatemala in the seventeenth and eighteenth centuries. Following an idea first outlined by Scholes and Roys (1968), he proposes that the word *Lacandon* is derived from *lacam tun,* or "great rock," the name of the Chol Maya fortress settlement on Lake Miramar. Significantly, the lake, the subject of a Spanish military expedition in 1559, was called "Lago de Lacandón" by the conquerors. According to this theory, Lacantun, which originally referred to the Chol inhabitants of the Lake Miramar community, was generalized to stand for any unpacified Indians in the area, thus supporting the connection between the two terms *Lacantun* and *Lacandon.*

A second theory, offered by Robert Bruce (1979:4) proposes that the word *Lacandon* was derived from the Mayan words *ah acantun,* or "to set up stone, stone pillars, or stone idols." Bruce writes: "*Ah acantun* would be a convenient term by which their [the Lacandones'] christianized Maya neighbors would call them 'the idolators,' 'the pagans,' or 'those who worship stones.' "

This explanation is supported by a variety of historical and archeological evidence. The "original" Lacandon were Chol-speaking Maya Indians. Early sources describing Chol religion say that they did not have idols, instead worshipping such natural phenomena as mountains. But the present-day Lacandon speak a dialect of Yucatecan Maya and pray and make offerings to clay "god pots," painted incense burners with the figures of their gods modeled on them. Thus, according to this theory, Lacandon was the name given to Yucatecan worshippers of idols by the native Chol peoples. The term was then adopted by the Spanish as a general name for the non-Christian Indians in Chiapas.

A preliminary fact that supports this immigration hypothesis is that the contemporary Lacandon speak a dialect of Yucatecan Maya while other Indian groups around them speak Tzeltal or Chol, all dialects of Maya but not so closely related as to be mutually intelligible. The Lacandon thus form a small island of Yucatecan-speaking people surrounded by a sea of Chol and Tzeltal speakers.

Historical records also indicate that the original inhabitants of the Lacandon jungle spoke Chol Maya. Tozzer (1913:497–509) cites a manuscript letter written in 1595 that contains a reference to Chol-speaking people in the area of the mission town of Dolores (exact site now unknown) in the jungle area south of Lake Miramar near the Lacantun river. Fr. Pedro Lorenzo, Bishop of Chiapas in 1560, was the man responsible for evangelizing and resettling the Indians in the area where the Lacandon live today. A skilled speaker of both Chol and Tzeltal Maya, Fr. Lorenzo traveled extensively in this area and did not mention the presence of Yucatecan-speaking people. Fr. Lorenzo also was responsible for the founding of the settlement of Pochutla, whose inhabitants were later transferred to Ocosingo, Tumbala, Tila, and Palenque. All these communities were populated by Chol-speaking Indians brought out of the surrounding jungle. Thus, it appears that the Lacandon came to this area after Lorenzo's work for the settlements that he founded, circling the Lacandon jungle on the south, west, and north. Yet, there is no record of contact with Yucatecan-speaking people at this time.

In 1646, Chol-speaking Franciscan missionaries sent for Yucatecan-speaking priests to work with a group of about 300 unconverted Yucatecan-speaking Indians concentrated in a settlement called Nohha. Nohha, which means "great water," was built on the shores of a lake and is described as being "about 15 or 18 leagues from Tenosique on the other side of the river" (Scholes and Roys 1968:45); in other words, it was roughly 50 miles south of Tenosique, which is approximately where the contemporary village of Najá, also built on a lake, is located.

Although not studied until the turn of this century, the presence of Yucatecan-speaking Lacandon in Chiapas has been sporadically document-ed by Spanish officials or European explorers since the seventeenth century. After the discovery of Nohha, the Lacandon drop from view until 1792–1793 when they are mentioned in a series of letters between the cura of Palenque, Manuel Joseph Calderón, and the Governor of Chiapas, concerning an armed uprising by the Lacandon in the jungle south of Palenque (Barlow 1943:158–159). (Incidentally, fifty years later, John L. Stephens heard the story of Calderón and his visit with the Lacandon while on a trip to the ruins at Palenque; the story is recounted in Stephens' book *Incidents of Travel in Central America, Chiapas, and Yucatán,* pp. 286–287.) Almost 100 years later, the German explorer Karl Sapper reported the presence of Lacandon in both northern and southern Lacandon jungle communities (Sapper 1897, reported in Nations 1979:100), and explorer Teobert Maler lived with a Lacandon family for one week in September 1898. The first anthropological work with the Lacandon was done by Alfred M. Tozzer, who stayed with a northern Lacandon family on two separate occasions in 1903 and 1904. Since that time, the Lacandon have been in semiregular contact with outsiders.

LACANDON ORIGINS AND MYTHOLOGY

What can the Lacandon themselves tell us about their origins? The hypoth-esis that the Lacandon immigrated from the Yucatán is supported by evidence found in the Lacandon myth "The Horses for the Lacandon." The Lacandon use this story to explain the technological differences between Lacandon and *ladino* (hispanicized Indian) society. In the myth, ladinos have steel tools, horses, livestock, and writing. Traditionally, the Lacandon have not had access to these things because, according to the story, the Lacandon did not take care of the gifts provided by Hachäkyum. Instead, these items are part of a different world, belonging to the people who live in towns. In fact, the term I have translated as ladinos, *kah,* literally means "townspeople." When examined from a historical perspective, the myth is also an accurate representation of the circumstances the Maya had forced upon them by the arrival of the Spaniards; it also embellishes the historical picture left us by sixteenth-century Spanish and Indian sources. Presented here is my translation of the myth as transcribed by Bruce (1974:137–145). The verse numbers are those used for identification in Bruce's Mayan transcription of the myth. Items in brackets are my additions to the text.

THE HORSES FOR THE LACANDON

1 Hachäkyum [the Lacandon creator deity] made horses for the Lacandon. Hachäkyum made horses.

2 He made cattle. He made pigs. He made dogs. He made cats, he made doves with chickens. He made them with Äkyantho' [the god of foreigners].

3 Äkyantho' made horses for the ladinos [Indians who adopt Mexican dress and habits]. He made cattle . . . Äkyantho' with Hachäkyum.

4 He made sheep, he made goats, he made dogs, he made cats, he made turkeys, he made chickens, he made pigs for the ladinos.

5 He created money for the authorities.

6 He made medicine. He made sickness with medicine. Hachäkyum did not make them. Äkyantho' made all the diseases. [Äkyantho' is also credited with the invention of writing and firearms.]

7 Äkyantho' and Hachäkyum finished their creations, they gave [these items] to the Lacandon.

8 Hachäkyum said "Here are horses; enclose them, guard them, water them, and feed them."

9 Here are pigs, pigs for you. For you chickens . . . turkeys. Take them all.

10 They [the Lacandon] took the animals and enclosed them. [But] they all escaped from the Lacandon. In the morning all were gone.

11 Äkyantho' gave them to the ladinos. "Here are horses, cattle, pigs, sheep, all for you. You guard them all."

12 The ladinos were good. They guarded them. They watched the pigs. They watched the horses and cattle.

13 They [the animals] were all tame, the ladinos guarded them all. They fed all the animals, they watered them.

14 Äkyantho' was happy. No animals escaped.

15 Hachäkyum said "Eh, you are very good. Horses will carry the ladinos . . . forever.

[16] Cattle are to pull out trees [use as draft animals]. There is wild game for eating." [Notice that as horses and cattle are new creations, humans must be told not to eat them and instructed in their correct usage.]

[17] Äkyantho' said to the ladinos "You may eat the flesh of cattle. Do not eat horses . . . they are for carrying things."

[18] [Äkyantho'] gave [ladinos] money. "For you pay people when they work for you."

[19] Äkyantho' said "In five days you untie your animals. Cattle you untie. Horses you untie. Pigs you untie . . . all of your animals. They will not escape. They are tame." After five days it was very good.

[20] Hachäkyum said "Eh, now I am not happy.

[21] Now there will be no [iron] machetes for them [the Lacandon]. No one will go to make machetes for them . . . no [steel] axes.

[22] They will search for stone [to make tools] to make their milpas.

[23] They will look for the ant mounds. They plant corn in the ant mounds.

[24] They will have arrows . . . no guns. They will have to make arrows with flint. They will go to search for flint." [In other words, Hachäkyum is saying that the Lacandon will be punished for losing their horses and cattle by not being granted objects such as steel tools, firearms, and the like.]

[25] Äkyantho' answered "No Lord. The Lacandon can buy machetes . . . for I will show the ladinos how to make all things."

[26] Hachäkyum answered "Eh good you. The cattle do not escape. Their animals do not escape. The ladinos will have all things.

[27] In five years they [the Lacandon] can go and buy [these items].

[28] They make arrows and sell them. They make arrows and sell them [for money to buy tools]. They will take axes . . . they take candles . . . and machetes. All things will they buy. Thus the Lacandon will have no money . . . forever."

[29] Hachäkyum said "Eh good, very good. It is good. There is salt. . . . Eh good. They will eat the ashes of the Kun [spined salt palm, *Acantorhiza moccini*]. . . . the ashes of wood."

The Lacandon believe Hachäkyum to be the creator of humankind and the earth as we know it today. In this capacity, he assumes responsibility for the welfare of the Lacandon. Äkyantho', on the other hand, is the god of foreigners—anyone who is not Indian. He dresses as a town dweller and is said to wear a hat and carry a pistol. He not only watches over foreigners but foreign animals and objects as well, so horses, cattle, pigs, metal tools, guns, and medicines are all under Äkyantho''s influence. Bruce (1967:96) adds to this list of attributes that Äkyantho² is also the god of money, and Tozzer (1907:94) says this god is associated with the north (it is common for Mayan peoples to associate various gods with the cardinal directions).

In this myth, Äkyantho² gives the ladinos objects such as horses and metal tools, unknown to the Maya until the arrival of the Spanish. One good example is the gift of *ta²k²in,* literally "excrement of the sun" (which refers specifically to gold and silver money) to the "authorities." But the Maya did not use a metal currency until the conquest. Throughout Mesoamerica, the cacao bean was the principle medium of exchange with jade and spondylus shell beads as secondary units of exchange (Thompson 1966:219).

In the myth, Äkyantho? is credited with the creation of diseases and the medicine to treat them. I do not believe it is a coincidence that the god of foreigners is believed to have created diseases that decimated the native population after their introduction by the Spanish. The previous discussion of Indian mortality rates from measles, smallpox, and yellow fever, all introduced by the Spanish, make that attribute of Äkyantho² quite clear. In fact, the Lacandon have suffered through a more recent version of this same process, beginning in the late nineteenth century and continuing to the present day. Isolated in the jungle of Chiapas, they missed many of the epidemics that previously swept through the Indian populations surrounding them. As Lacandon contact with outsiders (lumbermen and chicle workers) increased, so too did the incidence of infectious diseases. During the past 100 years, more than 50 percent of all known deaths have been caused by infectious diseases (Nations 1979:129); at one point, the Lacandon population declined to fewer than 100 individuals. Thus, the god of foreigners is linked to the introduction of foreign diseases just as foreigners have historically brought infectious diseases into the Lacandon jungle.

In the story, the Lacandon and ladinos are both given pigs, cattle, and horses, but the Lacandon do not care for their animals, allowing them to run away into the jungle as they sleep. As a consequence of this neglect, the Lacandon are not given metal tools and guns. They must work their fields with stone tools, hunt with bows and arrows, and sell crafts to make money so that they may buy goods from the ladinos.

This myth reflects actual historical circumstances. The Maya worked little metal, most of their metalcrafting being used for ornamentation while their tools were made of stone and wood. Similarly, in the myth, the god of foreigners gives town dwellers metal tools and guns while the Lacandon must obtain these objects from ladinos. Furthermore, the Indians of Mesoamerica had no large domesticated animals. The first cattle, horses, chickens, and pigs were all brought to the New World by the Spanish. Thus, in the myth, the god of foreigners, Äkyantho², is given credit for providing the very objects that in historical reality were introduced to the Indians by the conquering foreigners.

One last argument in support of a Yucatecan point of origin for the Lacandon is based on Lacandon mythic geography. The ancient Maya associated the four cardinal directions with different gods. The Lacandon retain this belief today and relate several of their gods to the four directions. One such association is made between Äkyantho² and the north. Although this may be coincidental, the route of the Spanish invasion of Chiapas from the Yucatán came from the north. Further, as Guatemala was subdued before Chiapas, a great deal of military traffic between Guatemala and Mexico traveled from north to south through Chiapas. For example, after Alvarado conquered Guatemala in April of 1524, he in turn had to be brought under control by Cortez, who marched an army from Mexico City through the jungle to Honduras (missing the ruins of Palenque by only a few miles!). It is improbable that the Lacandon were ignorant of this traffic. Thus, the Lacandon associate the god of foreigners with the north, the direction from which foreigners first came.* The myth, intentionally or not, accurately reflects the historical circumstances surrounding the Spanish conquest and supports the view that the Lacandon were originally from the Yucatán.

In the *Chilam Balam of Chumayel,* a Mayan book of history and prophecy written in 1782 (but copied verbatim from sixteenth- and seventeenth-century originals), is found the following eloquent statement:

> It was only because these priests of ours were come to an end when misery was introduced, when Christianity was introduced by the real Christians. Then with the true God, the true Dios, came the beginning of our misery. It was the beginning of strife with purse snatching, the beginning of strife with blowguns, the beginning of strife by trampling on people, the beginning of robbery with violence, the beginning of forced debts, the beginning of debts enforced by false testimony, the beginning of individual strife, a beginning of vexation, a beginning of robbery with violence. This was the origin of service to the Spanish and the priests . . . while the poor people were harassed. These were the very poor people who did not depart when oppression was put upon them (Roys, 1967:79).

The Spanish conquest of the Yucatán brought great hardship to the Maya people, and I believe that the ancestors of the contemporary Lacandon were among those Indians who departed when "oppression was put upon them."

Thus, the historical process by which the Lacandon came to Chiapas can be quickly summarized in the following stages:

1. The jungle of Chiapas was populated by Chol-speaking Indians before the conquest.

*Another bit of evidence suggesting a Yucatecan origin for the Lacandon is based on an analysis of the name Äkyantho², and was suggested to me in a review of an article I was writing. The reviewer commented that Äkyantho² may be derived from the Maya *äk yan Tiho²,* or, "our (Lord) in Mérida." At the very least, this suggests that the Lacandon at one time had a political relationship with the ruling hierarchy in the Yucatán.

2. The Choles were forcibly resettled into mission communities such as Dolores, Ocosingo, and Palenque by the Spanish clergy and military in the sixteenth and seventeenth centuries.

3. Forced resettlement of the Lacandon jungle created large areas of unpopulated land. As early as the mid-1600s, taking advantage of this opportunity, Yucatecan-speaking Maya Indians moved into the jungle areas south of Palenque and inherited the name Lacandon, a Mayan term adopted by the Spanish to refer to any non-Christian Indians in Chiapas.

4. The Yucatecan Lacandon lived largely undisturbed in the forests of southern Chiapas until the early twentieth century at which time Chol and Tzeltal Maya began to return to their ancestral homeland.

In conclusion, historical data supports the thesis presented here that the contemporary Lacandon are descendents of Yucatecan Maya Indians who fled the Yucatán for the jungle of Chiapas in the seventeenth and eighteenth centuries, to escape the effects of the Spanish invasion and occupation of the Yucatán peninsula.

Having provided a historical context to our study of the Lacandon let us now turn to the contemporary people. In the following chapter we will begin with an examination of the social organization of the Lacandon of Najá.

CHAPTER THREE

🐚 Social Organization in Najá

Approximately ninety people live in Najá today. This is approximate because the Lacandon's high birth and infant mortality rates make it difficult to keep an accurate record of births and deaths of small children in the community. The actual population of the area is greater, for there are Lacandon families and small groups of non-Lacandon Indians living in relative seclusion in the jungle around the village, but these people are not included in the data presented below. Table 3.1 shows the breakdown of the population in Najá by age, but this information is based only on my estimates. The Lacandon know the relative ages of everyone in the village—in other words, the order in which people were born—but they themselves do not keep track of their chronological ages and their self-estimates of age vary wildly. For example, a parent will guess that his obviously adolescent child is "six years old."

Polygyny, although not common, is still occasionally practiced among the people of Najá as it was in Mensäbäk and Lacanha before their conversion to Protestant Christianity. In Najá, only two men have more than one wife, and these two are the oldest and most respected men of the community. Although the households of these two men run smoothly, multiple wives in a household may cause problems. Nations (1979) describes several cases of young (teenage) co-wives in Mensäbäk who were starved and beaten by an older wife in the household. Despite the potential for conflict, animosity in a household is kept to a minimum by the practice of sororal polygyny. In this practice, a man's second wife is often his first wife's younger sister. Even in households where co-wives are not related, fictive kin relationships may be assigned. For example, in one polygynous household in Najá where the women are not related, co-wives still address each other as "sister," thus keeping jealousy and competition to a minimum. When questioned, women in this polygynous household said they got along well together in sharing the workload of the household and taking care of their husband and children. In this family, they even alternate cooking days to ensure that kitchen duties are evenly rotated.

The family structure in a household with multiple wives is not communal even though living quarters are shared. It is more accurate to describe these households as distinct family units united only through the husband/father, who is the head of the household. Although the wives

TABLE 3.1 *Age distribution in Najá*

	0–1	1–9	10–19	20–39	over 40	over 60
F	7	19	5	11	3	1
M	6	14	5	16	2	1

divide the workload of their combined household, each wife is in charge of her own children. Responsibility for the feeding and care of children is not shared.

In many Mayan societies, men do the majority of work in the milpa as well as hunt, thus providing a major percentage of the food protein, while women handle virtually all domestic chores. For example, among the Maya in the highlands of Guatemala, milpa work is men's work and only the poorest of families employ the labor of women in the fields. This is not true in Najá, where the work load is fairly evenly shared between men and women. Ideally, men conduct the heavy work in the milpa, in particular, cutting, clearing, and burning the fields before planting. They also hunt, and concern themselves with the spiritual well-being of their families for religious activities are almost entirely a male responsibility. The principal tasks of women, on the other hand, are primarily domestic. They care for the home, children, and poultry, and prepare food. Lacandon men joke that they would starve to death without a woman to prepare their meals, and they see food preparation as a principal reason to marry. Yet despite this ideal division of labor in Najá, the responsibilities of men and women overlap a great deal. Planting, weeding, and harvesting crops in the milpa are tasks shared by Lacandon men and women. Hunting, a traditionally male activity, is also one in which the women share. It is not uncommon for a woman to accompany her husband on a hunting trip. Finally, caring for children, ideally the work of women, is also shared among family members. It is quite common for both boys and girls to watch their younger siblings.

Children in Lacandon families accept household responsibilities at an early age. As soon as boys are old enough to swing a machete, they begin helping with work in the milpa, gathering firewood, and fishing. A special treat for young men is to go hunting with their fathers and be allowed to handle firearms. By the age of eight or nine, young girls are caring for their younger siblings, carrying them slung in a scarf tied over one shoulder while they do their household chores. Children old enough to walk fend for themselves, learning adult roles and responsibilities by imitating their parents and older siblings. There is little formal instruction in this society. Children learn by watching adults and are capable of working like adults at an early age. Furthermore, there is no real period of adolescence. In American society, the teenage years are a time of transition from childhood to adulthood. The markers of this transition are events such as getting a driver's license, a first job, and graduating from high school. In the Lacandon Jungle, Indian children have assumed the tasks of an adult, be it making a milpa or caring for children, by the time they are in their early teens.

MARRIAGE AND ADULTHOOD

In virtually all societies around the world, marriage is the event that marks the change from adolescent to adult status. Similarly, a Lacandon man and woman are not considered fully adult until they are married and have children. By the time she reaches her early teens, a Lacandon woman is considered to have attained marriageable age, and most women marry soon after puberty. Child brides, although uncommon, are not unknown. In this situation, a man must be content to raise a young girl until she is old enough to bear children and care for a home. Lacandon men, on the other hand, start thinking about marriage around the age of sixteen, and are generally married and fathers by the time they reach nineteen or twenty.

The Lacandon definition of adulthood puts me, as a thirty-three-year-old unmarried man, in a curious position in the village. One of the first questions asked upon my periodic return trips to Najá is whether I have married, and the Lacandon do not understood how I could conduct the business of adulthood without a wife and children. This role confusion was neatly summed up in a statement by a young man about ten years younger than I. He said, "You have more years than I do, but I am more mature because I have a wife and two children."

This situation has also resulted in a joke (at my expense) that has survived since 1982 and is inevitably brought up in my presence during visits to Najá. One young Lacandon wit suggested that I should marry his friend's maternal grandmother, a very old woman. After all, he reasoned, I need a wife and she needs a husband. In the standard joke, this suggestion is followed by a discussion of the benefits of our marriage, which include her cooking for me, washing my clothes, and, of course, sexual favors. My denials of interest in this woman are met only with more intense (and personal) suggestions about how to conduct the courtship. After years of trying to defend myself against this joke I have just about given up.

When a Lacandon man decides he is ready to marry, he first makes his own milpa to demonstrate his ability to support a family. He then enters a protracted set of negotiations with the father of the girl he has chosen as a potential spouse. A young man regularly visits the household of his prospective father-in-law, bringing small gifts such as tobacco, cloth, or food. But any attempt to discuss marriage will be rebuffed by the girl's father, who may describe her as lazy and unfit to marry. This running argument may go on for a year before the girl's father finally gives his consent for the marriage. Thus, a young man must prove both his industry and persistence before he can marry.

Once a marriage is agreed upon, there is no formal ceremony. A man simply moves into his father-in-law's household and begins a period of bride service that may last from a few months to a couple of years. A man pays for his bride by working in her parents' household, hunting for this family, and working in his father-in-law's milpas. Traditionally, when his bride service was completed, a man returned to live near his father's household, but this pattern has changed in recent years. Several young men who married into Najá families have chosen to remain there, living with their wife's family even though they have fulfilled their bride service obligations.

A newly married couple will live first with the bride's parents, but once the young couple begins to have children, generally when the wife is about sixteen, the young man constructs a separate residence in his father-in-law's compound. Thus, in Najá, one finds a variable pattern of patrilocal and matrilocal postmarital residence.

RESIDENTIAL PATTERNS

Residence in Lacandon villages is based on the household cluster, a group of homes built together because of the relationships shared by the occupants. Najá can be divided into five such clusters, with young men building households around the home of either their fathers or fathers-in-law (see Table 3.2). These clusters are formed by:

1. The households of Chan K'in Viejo, one of his sons and three of his sons-in-law
2. The households of Mateo Viejo, two of his sons, and three of his sons-in-law
3. The households of Antonio and two of his sons-in-law
4. The households of Mateo Joven and his son-in-law
5. The "Independents," four households that are composed of the sons-in-law of a man who is now dead.

The relationship among these households illustrates the mix of post-marital residential practices current in Najá and the interrelationship among clusters. In Chan K'in Viejo's cluster are found one of his sons (patrilocal postmarital residence) and three of his sons-in-law (matrilocal postmarital residence). Mateo Viejo's cluster illustrates this same pattern. Further, Mateo's oldest son-in-law is one of Chan K'in Viejo's sons. Antonio is Chan K'in Viejo's oldest son-in-law; Antonio's sons-in-law are Chan K'in Viejo's sons. Mateo Joven, who is Mateo Viejo's oldest son, formed his own household cluster when he gave one of his infant daughters in marriage to a young man who then built a house near his new father-in-law. Thus, Mateo Joven and his son-in-law are very nearly the same age. The in-

TABLE 3.2 *Organization of households in Najá*

1. THE COMPOUND OF CHAN K'IN VIEJO

Chan K'in Viejo's household

Chan K'in Joven's household (son of Chan K'in Viejo)

Paco's household (son-in-law of Chan K'in Viejo)

K'in Panni-Agua's household (son-in-law of Chan K'in Viejo)

Bol's household (son-in-law of Chan K'in Viejo)

K'in's household (son of Chan K'in Viejo)

2. THE COMPOUND OF MATEO VIEJO

Mateo Viejo's household

K'in's household (younger son of Mateo Viejo)

Nuxi's household (son-in-law of Mateo Viejo)

Kayum's household (son-in-law of Mateo Viejo)

K'in's household (son-in-law of Mateo Viejo)

Kayum's household (son of Mateo Viejo)

3. THE COMPOUND OF ANTONIO

Antonio's household

Kayum's household (son-in-law of Antonio)

Bol's household (son-in-law of Antonio, younger brother of Kayum)

4. THE COMPOUND OF MATEO JOVEN (MATEO VIEJO'S SON)

Mateo Joven's household

Juan Jose's household (son-in-law of Mateo Joven)

5. THE INDEPENDENTS (SONS-IN-LAW OF JOSE GUERO, WHO DIED IN 1977)

Jose Celosa's household

Chan K'in's household

Pepe Vasquez's household

Chan K'in's household

---

dividuals whom I call the Independents live together in the same cluster because, with one exception, they are all married to daughters of a man who died in 1977. They are simply following the pattern found in the other clusters, sons-in-law living near their fathers-in-law, except that their father-in-law is dead.

KINSHIP AND NAMES

If this all seems confusing to an outsider, it only gets worse when we attempt to refer to specific Lacandon individuals by name. The Lacandon use only a few proper names. Although some adopt Mexican names such as Mateo or Antonio, in standard Lacandon practice all men are named Nuxi, Kʼin, Bol, or Kayum, and all women are named either Koh or Nuk. *Chan,* meaning "little," may be used before any of these names to provide some variety, but the system can still confuse visitors. For example, naming Chan Kʼin Viejo's children living in Najá, from oldest to youngest, provides the following list: Kʼin, Chan Kʼin, Chan Nuk, Nuk, Koh, Kayum, Chan Kʼin, Bol, Kʼin, Chan Nuk, Chan Kʼin, Chan Bol, Chan Kayum, Chan Kʼin, Kʼin, and Chan Nuk. Thus, it is difficult to identify particular people by reference only to their name. Walking out into the village and calling "Chan Kʼin" might elicit a response from twenty different individuals.

Although the Lacandon use personal names in family situations (context usually makes clear who is being addressed), an elaborate set of kin terms is more commonly used to refer to specific individuals or to address others in the community. For instance, in conversation I might refer to an individual as *Kʼin u tial Chan Kʼin, u sukun Kayum,* or "Kʼin the son of Chan Kʼin and the older brother of Kayum," to name a specific individual. This may seem cumbersome to us, but a Lacandon can name anyone virtually instantly by reference to a specific kin term.* Therefore, to follow a conversation, it is necessary to understand Lacandon relationship terminology. Table 3.3, taken from Boremanse (1977–78), lists the common set of terms used by the Lacandon.

Using these kin terms is not as difficult as it seems. For example, if I am referring to my wife, I say, *In lak* ("my wife"), whereas if I call someone my *Naʼ,* then I could be addressing my mother, my mother's sister, my father's brother's wife, or my son's wife. The context of the conversation would make clear who was being discussed.

One concept that was important in Lacandon marriages but has little significance today is the *onen.* The onen is an animal name, inherited from one's father, which today is used as a surname. Chan Kʼin Viejo (and thus all of his children), for example, is of the *maʼax* ("spider monkey") onen. Thus, his proper name, the one used in documents, is Chan Kʼin Maʼax. Bruce (1979:20) believes that the Lacandon once practiced onen endogamous marriages, but a severe reduction in the Lacandon population in the first part of this century led to a breakdown of the rule. For those interested in pursuing this idea, Boremanse (1978:366–368) provides a statistical breakdown of Lacandon marriages by onen; today, however, this concept is not important. I heard discussions of onen usually in reference to dream analysis, where dreaming of an animal actually

---

*This topic was the subject of a dissertation by Rees (1978), who created a mathematical model duplicating the logical process that a Lacandon individual follows when identifying others with this kin terminology.

TABLE 3.3 *Lacandon kin terms (male ego)*

TERMS OF REFERENCE ONLY

Lak: spouse

Tial or Pa'al-al: either son or daughter

Haan: daughter's husband

TERMS OF REFERENCE OR ADDRESS

Tet: father or stepfather

Yum: FB, BS, MZH, FBSS, MZSS, FFBS, FMZS, MH

Ixkit: yB, yZ, yFBS, yFBD, yMZS, yMZD, SS, SD, yMBSW, yFZSW, yWZH

Sukun: eB, eFBS, eMZS, FF, FFB, eWZH

Kik: eZ, eFBD, eMZD, eMBSW, eFZSW, eWBW

Chiich: MM, MMZ

Na': M, MZ, FBW, SW

Ts'ena': ZD, MDSD, FZSD, FBDD, MZDD, WBD

Akan: MB, ZS, FZH, WF, MBSS, FZSS, FBDS, MZDS, WBS, FMBS, FFZS

Mäm: WB, ZH, MBS, MBD, FZS, FZD, MF, DS, DD

Mim: FM

Mu: WZ, BW

Key to abbreviations
y refers to younger, e to elder

B = brother	D = daughter	F = father
H = husband	M = mother	S = son
W = wife	Z = sister	

For example, eZ = elder sister and MBS = mother's brother's son.

refers to a person of that onen. For example, to dream of a spider monkey could mean that you would soon see a person of the ma'ax onen.

The Lacandon recognize several different onen, all of which have a common animal name or two, plus a ceremonial name (see Table 3.4). The onen is often compared to other systems of human and animal classification such as totemism and nagualism, although, strictly speaking, it is not. A person's onen is not his totem because the Lacandon do not believe they are descended from these animals; in addition, there are no taboos about eating the animal represented by one's onen. Furthermore,

TABLE 3.4 *Lacandon onen*

CEREMONIAL NAME	COMMON NAME
Kasyho²	Ma²ax: spider monkey Ba²ats: howler monkey
Koho²	K²ek²en: white-lipped peccary Kitam: collared peccary
Keho²	Yuk: white-tailed deer Keh: mule deer
Nahwahto²	K²ambul: curassow Koox: wild turkey
Haawo²	Ak²äbäk: raccoon Ts²uts²u: coatimundi
Nistisyaho²	Hale: paca Tsup: prairie dog
Kobaho²	Chilu: quail
Witso²	Hunk²uk²: eagle
Puko²	Balum: jaguar Chäk Balum: puma
Taxo²	Sa²hol: badger
Uuko²	Uuk: dove Ts²ul: dove
Miso²	Mo²: macaw Ka²cho or T²ut²: parrot

From Bruce, Robert D. (1979: 21)

the onen is not a nagual because humans do not transform themselves into these animals. Although other Indian groups in the area do believe in naguales, the Lacandon claim that these are merely their onen.

According to Bruce (1979:22), all known living Lacandon belong to only four onen. The northern Lacandon possess two onens, *ma²ax* and *k²ek²en* (spider monkey and peccary), while the southern Lacandon have three, *k²ek²en, yuk,* and *k²ambul* (peccary, deer, and curassow). Chan K²in Viejo's mother is said to have belonged to the *ak²äbäk* (raccoon) onen, but all members of other onen either have been assimilated into Mexican society and dropped the association or have died.

The Lacandon gods also have onen, although they belong to only three, *ma²ax, k²ek²en,* and *yuk.* Table 3.5, based on information supplied in the

TABLE 3.5 *Classification of Lacandon gods by onen*

MA'AX ONEN	K'EK'EN ONEN
Hachäkyum	Mensäbäk
Itzanal	Ts'ibatnah
Ak'inchob	Itzanok'uh
Säkäpuk	Känäk'ax
K'ulel	
Bol	YUK ONEN
K'ayum	Ah K'ak'
K'in	

Lacandon myth of the creation of the gods from the *bäk nikte'* flower (see Bruce 1974:25–34), illustrates this division.

The Lacandon believe that all human beings have onen, including foreigners. If we do not know our onen affiliation, this is merely a sign that we have forgotten our traditions. Interviewing individuals about their onen generally resulted in questions about mine. When I responded that I did not know what my onen was, friends speculated that it must be *Miso'*. They reasoned that my name, Juan, was linguistically similar to the Maya word *ah wan* ("partridge"), a bird similar to the macaw and parrot, which forms the Miso' onen. Furthermore, because of the similarity in the sound of the words Juan and wan (partridge), making puns based on the two became a common activity in public situations. For example, Mateo Viejo would joke that he was going to kill, pluck, and eat me with tortillas.

Having now described the various roles of Lacandon men and women, their social structure, and community organization, in the next chapter I turn to a brief discussion of Lacandon subsistence practices and material culture.

CHAPTER FOUR

🦂 Lacandon Subsistence and Economics

The Lacandon live in tropical rainforest, and literally cut their living out of this forest. Although some have called these jungles "protein deserts" because of the highly dispersed populations of local fauna (see Nigh and Nations 1980:17), when the proper techniques are employed, the jungle is capable of supporting large populations of people. The Lacandon are masters at using the jungle's resources without over exploiting and damaging their environmental surroundings. In this chapter, I will illustrate the process the Lacandon use to provide themselves with abundant food supplies while at the same time maintaining a harmony with their environment, practices in sharp contrast to the destruction caused by the agricultural techniques and livestock production of their Indian neighbors.

Currently, many rainforest farmers clear large tracts of land but do not allow the forest to lie fallow after the nutrients in the soil are depleted. Instead, the land is seeded with grasses so that cattle may be grazed on it and sold in the commercial beef industry. This practice upsets the finely balanced nutrient levels in the soil and greatly increases soil erosion. In particular, water erosion becomes a problem in rainforest areas that have been cleared because of the heavy rainfall. Land abused in this fashion cannot easily return to forest, and huge expanses of former jungle have been turned into what Geertz (1963:25) called a "green desert" in describing this process in Southeast Asia.

Contrary to the practice described above, the Lacandon treat the jungle as a renewable resource and follow a subsistence strategy that permits them to use several food-producing zones within the forest. The three most important zones of food production are the pristine forest, milpa (cultivated fields), and *acahuales,* or milpas that have been abandoned and left to regenerate to forest.*

The principal form of Lacandon agricultural production is swidden, or slash-and-burn, agriculture. The first step in this process is for a Lacandon farmer to choose a site for his milpa. He selects land with the appropriate soil and drainage by checking the natural vegetation growing on the milpa

*Much of the information presented in this chapter is derived from a fascinating article on the Lacandon milpa system by Nations and Nigh (1980).

site. It is desirable to cut a milpa on land where the breadnut tree *(Trophis mexicana)* and the ceiba tree *(Ceiba pentandra)* grow because these trees flourish on rich soils that will produce a good harvest. On the other hand, Lacandon farmers avoid areas where mahogany and tropical cedar grow because they are too wet.

The Lacandon usually cut milpas in acahuales that have been left fallow generally from ten to twenty years. Although the benefit of clearing a milpa in primary forest is high, with a first year production of up to six tons of shelled corn per hectare (Nations and Nigh 1980), it also takes a great deal more work. Where a man can clear one hectare of regrowth in about eight days of work, the same size tract of pristine forest takes thirty to forty days. Given the extra effort required to cut primary forest, a Lacandon man generally cuts primary forest only on one side of his milpa and allows the opposite edge of the field to go fallow in a process similar to that described by Chagnon for the Yanomamö (1977:35). The farmer then plants tree crops such as bananas in the fallowed field so that even if a garden is no longer actively worked it will continue to produce food. Thus, a continuing forest–milpa–fallow cycle is created in which food production can be maintained at all three stages of the cycle.

The preparation of a milpa begins when a farmer clears all plant growth from a selected site. This work is done by hand, using machete and axe. The trees and underbrush of a new field are cut during January, February, or March, then allowed to dry. In mid-April or early May (just before the rainy season begins), this dry underbrush is burned, depositing a layer of fertilizing ash over the milpa. This method of horticulture is particularly effective in tropical forests because of the distribution of nutrients in rainforest ecosystems. In temperate forests, such as those in the United States, the majority of nutrients are found in their soils. On the other hand, 75 percent of the nutrients in a tropical environment are contained in the forest's living biomass, with only some 8 percent of a rainforest's nutrients contained in the soil. Thus, burning the dried brush in a field is an effective means of placing the forest's nutrients in the soil where they can be used by the farmer's food crops.

Once a field is burned, the farmer may wait up to a month before planting his main crop (corn), for he has to coordinate planting with the onset of the seasonal rains in June. Yet a farmer is not idle during this period, for he can sow both root and tree crops such as manioc, chayote, and bananas. When the rains begin, the Lacandon farmer plants his milpa with corn, beans, and squash. The Lacandon do not till their fields; a digging stick is the principal tool used in planting. To sow his crops, a farmer simply pokes a hole in the ground with his digging stick and drops seed into this hole. About two weeks after planting, a farmer reseeds areas that have failed to germinate.

Planting continues during the rainy season, for the Lacandon cultivate a wide variety of root and vegetable crops. Among the many vegetable foods grown in the milpa are onions, lemon grass, jicamas, tomatoes, two different types of beans, chili, garlic, yams, avocado, sugar cane, and mint. Several fruits also are cultivated, including pineapple, custard apple, watermelon, limes, oranges, grapefruit, and bananas. Although the Lacandon have no knowledge of the Prehispanic Mayan ritual calendar that governed the seasons for planting (and in simplified form is still followed by some Mayan peoples; for example, see Redfield, 1976), planting periods for crops are determined by the flowering of specific species of forest plants. This form of timing, as Nations and Nigh (1980) note, carefully coordinates the planting cycle with current environmental conditions.

Once the corn begins to sprout, the most arduous work in the milpa is weeding. Weeds are not a problem in a newly cut milpa but they do become a nuisance by the field's second or third year of use. In fact, proliferation of weeds and declining yields are the two principal reasons for abandoning a milpa and clearing a new field. Otherwise, a family has to spend several hours a day pulling weeds by hand or cutting them with a machete. Having participated in all phases of the milpa cycle, this is most certainly the task I least enjoyed.

Although a Lacandon farmer may cultivate forty to fifty different plant species, a viewer's dominant impression of a milpa will be of corn because a farmer disperses his crops widely over the field. As Nations and Nigh (1980:11) write, "Although the milpa may contain twenty bunches of onion plants, none of these bunches will be situated within three meters of another." Distributing a variety of plants over a milpa, without clustering bunches of plants together, has the practical effect of imitating the diversity and dispersal of plant life found in an undisturbed primary forest. In contrast to monocrop agriculture as practiced in the United States, the milpa attempts to maintain rather than replace the structure of the tropical rainforest ecosystem. In effect, the milpa is a portion of jungle where a greater than normal population of food-producing crops has been concentrated. This concentration of food is aided by the fact that Lacandon farmers plant their milpas with crops that take advantage of different environmental niches within the same cleared area. For example, at ground level, hills of corn, beans, squash, and tomatoes are sown. A few meters above the surface grow tree crops such as bananas and oranges, and, finally, subsurface root crops such as manioc and sweet potatoes are cultivated below the ground's surface. Thus, a Lacandon farmer achieves at least three levels of production from the same piece of land.

In the late fall as the corn ripens, a farmer comes to his milpa every few days, picking just enough corn to fill his family's immediate needs. There is usually no large-scale harvesting effort. Instead, ears of corn are left on the stalk but bent pointing downward so that rain does not seep through the husks and mold the ears. At this time, preparation also begins for planting a second maize crop because the climate is mild and the soil rich enough to support two plantings a year. Yield estimates compiled by Nations and Nigh (1980:13) for the Lacandon community of Lacanha Chan Sayab indicate that the Lacandon milpa produces an abundant harvest, approximately

2.8 metric tons of shelled corn per hectare (after animal and pest losses). Coupled to this yield estimate is the fact that under swidden agriculture it is estimated to take an average of 143 to 161 man-days of required labor per year to produce these yields (Adams 1973:43). In other words, a Lacandon family has to work in its milpas about half a year to feed itself for a complete year. The rest of the time can thus be spent in other pursuits such as hunting or leisure time activities that contribute to the household economy, for example, bow and arrow making.

While living in Najá, I worked with Chan K'in Viejo's family in its milpa. Because of my woeful ignorance of plants in Lacandon gardens, a young boy was usually assigned to work with me and keep me from accidentally cutting down useful cultigens with indiscriminate swipes of my machete. Although weeding a milpa on hot sunny days was not one of my favorite tasks, it did have its moments of excitement. I vividly remember leading a stampede out of the milpa one morning after my young chaperone accidently whacked a hornets' nest that was hidden in a clump of weeds. Having sprinted out of harm's way I turned to watch in admiration as this boy, wielding his machete like a baseball bat, took up a batting stance Babe Ruth would have appreciated, and began swatting hornets out of the air. Although I respected his bravery, he won a Pyrrhic victory. Several painful stings were the final result of his duel with the hornets.

The second subsistence zone used by the Lacandon is the acahual, or milpa left fallow. As described above, Lacandon farmers often plant fruit trees in abandoned milpas and continue to harvest leftover plant crops and species of wild plants from the acahual. Thus, the milpa is not really abandoned, for it continues to be an important source of vegetable foods for Lacandon families.

Although important as a source of vegetable foods, the fallowed milpa has an even more important role in Lacandon subsistence: it attracts game animals who come there to forage. The abandoned milpa has a greater concentration of food sources than the surrounding jungle and once it is no longer actively occupied by human beings it becomes an attractive source of food for game. Acahuales become what Nations and Nigh calls a "managed wildlife area" (1980:15). The abandoned milpa provides a food supplement that allows for a greater population of game animals. In turn, these animals become an indispensable source of high quality animal protein for the Lacandon. In this way, the abandoned milpa allows the forest to regenerate, attracts and feeds populations of game animals, and provides game that supplements the Lacandon's vegetable diet (see Table 4.1).

The final subsistence ecozone utilized by the Lacandon is the primary forest, which yields a wide variety of plant and animal resources. The forest is a source of both food and raw materials for construction (wood for beams, thatch for roofing), tools (wood for bow and arrows, feathers for fletching, flint for projectile points and blades, plant fiber for twine), and crafts (clay for pottery, mineral and vegetable pigments for dyes,

TABLE 4.1 *Common Lacandon game animals that feed in the acahual*

ENGLISH	LACANDON
Agouti	Tsup
Armadillo	Wech
Brocket deer	Yuk
Collared peccary	Kitam
Opossum	Och
Paca	Háale
Parrot	T'ut'
Rabbit	T'ul
Raccoon	Ak'äbäk
Squirrel	Kúuk
White-tailed deer	Keh

feathers for decoration). Local lakes provide fish, shellfish, turtles and turtle eggs, snails, and occasional crocodiles as yet other sources of nutrition. Table 4.2 (taken from Nations and Nigh 1980) provides a partial list of some of the plant resources found in the jungle and includes the uses of these plants.

Swidden horticulture is the means by which the Lacandon transform natural forest into "harvestable forest" (Geertz 1963:25). It is clear that the average Lacandon farmer has a great deal to teach industrial societies about productive methods for taking advantage of tropical forest products without destroying these resources. Before I make the Lacandon sound like environmental activists, let me also describe their appetite for material goods, for an equally important feature of contemporary Lacandon society is their desire to acquire modern technology.

TECHNOLOGICAL CHANGES

One of the visually obvious advances in Lacandon technology is in the construction of their dwellings. Lacandon house-building techniques have undergone tremendous innovation in the last ten years. The traditional dirt-floored, thatch-roofed hut, often built without walls, has largely been replaced by wooden-walled huts with cement floors and tin roofs. In 1982, a government-sponsored house-building program provided the opportu-

TABLE 4.2 *Some useful plants of the primary forest*

ENGLISH	LACANDON	USE
Spined salt palm	Kun	Source of salt
Breadnut	Hach ox	Fruit
Mamey	Háas	Fruit
Guatapil palm	Paho	Roofing
Wild clove	Pesa	Condiment
Balche	Balché	Bark for ritual beverage
Sapodilla	Hach ya	Fruit
Passion fruit	Chun ak$^?$	Fruit
Wild avocado	On	Fruit
Guava	Pichik, pul	Fruit
Pomegranate	U p$^?$uk tsup	Fruit
Copal	Pom	Incense
Wild cacao	Balum té	Condiment for beverages
Bayo	Tzayok	Roof beams
Barí	Bahbah	Latex sealer for bark cloth
Chimon tree	Chukun	Cure for toothache
Tropical cedar	K$^?$uh che	Arrow shafts
Amate	Moak té	Medicine for diarrhea
Poisonwood	Chechem	Fish poison
Basket vine	Ilo	Material for baskets
Pitch pine	Täte	Incense and illumination
Mahogany	Puuna	Canoes and Furniture

nity for even greater change, supplying the materials for cinder-block houses. The three men who took advantage of this offer now own two-room, whitewashed, cement-block houses. However, the owners use these homes principally for storage, because they have doors that can be locked and are thus secure from intrusion by outsiders traveling through Najá.

Following the traditional Lacandon pattern, most everyday activities such as eating, visiting, and cooking are conducted in wooden huts built near their cinder-block houses.

As a community, the people of Najá own three automobiles, two pickups and a three-quarter-ton truck, given to them through the office of the governor of Chiapas. These trucks are used mainly for transportation to and from nearby villages. Although ostensibly communally owned, only two men in Najá know how to drive and thus they exercise a monopoly over use of the vehicles. For example, as owner of the town store, the president of Najá reserves the use of one truck largely for hauling supplies for his store as well as for conducting community affairs. In this dual role as storekeeper and village business officer, he travels quite a bit between Tuxtla, the capital of the state of Chiapas, San Cristobal, and Palenque, often being gone for several days a week.

Lacandon men have a tremendous urge to acquire new technology (starting with metal tools and graduating to objects such as chain saws), although they do not have the equipment or technological knowledge necessary to maintain these items. One young man, for instance, recently purchased a gas stove, although he did not have the bottled gas necessary to use it. His wife still cooks over a traditional wood fire like the rest of the women in Najá. A more common example of the Lacandon's fascination with technology is that most adult men wear wristwatches. Although few men can read them and time is usually judged by the position of the sun, the watch is seen as a desirable and prestigious possession.

A recent example of this attraction to novel technology occurred during my visit to Najá in the winter of 1985. I was attempting to make a photographic census of the village using a Polaroid instant camera. Going from household to household, I took two sets of photographs, one for my census and the other for the people in the picture. During this exercise, I received two different requests to purchase the camera, although it is impossible to buy the necessary film packs within at least 100 square miles of the village. As far as I know, the special film required for this camera may only purchased in larger Mexican cities. Still, this fact did not deter the men's desire to acquire my camera, and my refusal to sell it remained fresh in the mind of one individual three years after this incident. Because of its uniqueness, the camera was viewed as a highly desirable item even if it could not be used to take photographs. These brief examples illustrate the striking mix of traditional and modern influences that characterize Lacandon society today. How this technological curiosity will affect their life-style and environment in the long run remains an open question.

Many of the technological changes in the Lacandon life-style have been made possible by the fact that they have become, relatively speaking, wealthy from the sale of lumbering rights to their land and craftworks to tourists. According to Boremanse (1978:5), in August 1975, the head of each Lacandon family received 4,862 pesos (about $195 U.S.); in November 1975, 6,060 pesos more (about $240 U.S.), and

By November, 1975, the Lacandon as a group had received credit from la Nacional Financiera for five million pesos of a contracted seven million in exchange for lumbering rights within their national territory. The bulk sum has been placed in a group fund controlled by the 'Fondo Nacional de Fomento Ejidal' (National Fund for the Promotion of Communal Territories).

This money has been spent to construct several clinics in the Lacandon Jungle as well as a small grocery store in each Lacandon community, stores that sell items not readily available in the jungle such as soap, rice, batteries, cigarettes, and canned goods. The stores were formerly stocked with goods bought with money from this government fund, according to Nations and Nigh (1979:117). Today, they are run as private businesses by individual Lacandon men.

Cash payments from the lumber companies are no longer an important source of income in Lacandon households. The most lucrative lumber resource in this area was mahogany, but as their stands in the Lacandon Jungle have declined, so too have payments to each household. I witnessed the distribution of lumber company royalties several times, and they never totaled more than a few hundred pesos to each Lacandon family. (This is even more true today with the drastic devaluation of the Mexican peso. At the time of this writing, the official exchange rate is more than 2,000 pesos per U.S. dollar.) Today, instead of lumber money, the primary source of income is from the sale of bow-and-arrow sets and pottery to tourists visiting the ruins of Palenque and the city of San Cristobal De Las Casas. The construction of these items, which is a leisure time activity that does not detract from traditional subsistence activities, can bring a surprisingly large sum of money to an industrious person. In one weekend at Palenque, I witnessed one young man sell 200 bow-and-arrow sets (Figure 4.1). Charging 500 pesos a set, he sold them all in three days, thus earning 100,000 pesos or about $670 U.S. (at the 1982 exchange rate). One week later, a second young man sold another 150 bow-and-arrow sets. Since this time, prices have gone steadily upward. The price of a bow-and-arrow set in 1985 was 1,000 pesos, and in 1988 the price had risen to 10,000 pesos a set. In this manner, Lacandon men have established a lucrative part-time profession. Furthermore, when sales are slow at nearby ruins, enterprising young men travel substantial distances in search of buyers for their crafts. I have seen Lacandon selling their bows and arrows in Mérida, Yucatán, and have heard reports of young men traveling as far north as the state of Chihuahua.

Although they universally claim to be broke, it is not uncommon for Lacandon men to have a great deal of cash on hand. This led to awkward confrontations on a couple of occasions when men approached me asking for loans. They assumed that because I was a tsul (a light-skinned foreigner) with a camera and tape recorder, I must be rich. In fact, as a graduate student supported only by a research grant, I had very little

FIGURE 4.1 *A Lacandon man selling bow-and-arrow sets at the ruins of Palenque*

money. Paradoxically, many Lacandon men had more money than I did, and I was also afraid if I lent money to one individual I would be besieged with requests for loans from others.

The money earned in the sale of items to tourists is usually used for household goods such as canned foods, cloth, and kitchen utensils. But on at least two occasions, these large sums of money have been important to the survival of Lacandon families. In the fall of 1982 and again in the spring of 1983, several families in Najá suffered failures of their corn crop. Their ability to earn large sums of money enabled these people to buy corn when their own crops had failed and thus survive until the second planting of corn in their milpas had matured. In one instance, a Lacandon man in Najá bought the complete corn crop of a milpa that was owned by a man from Mensäbäk. With this man's sons and friends, I spent a day transferring the corn from the milpa near Mensäbäk to the buyer's home in Najá. More recently, Chan Kʔin Viejo has hired a Tzeltal Mayan man to do the heavy work in his milpa. Chan Kʔin is very old and frail, and his unmarried sons too young to carry out this work for him. Thus, the income derived from his family's sale of crafts to tourists allows Chan Kʔin to continue to support his family.

This capability to produce income, bemoaned by Boremanse (1981) and Perera (1988), from one point of view has provided an alternate strategy with which the Lacandon can adapt to the uncertainties of their environment. Still, this ability to earn money is admittedly a mixed blessing. Although this income has provided a degree of flexibility in the subsistence practices of Lacandon families, it also has had negative consequences. The ability to purchase packaged foods such as rice, beans, refined sugar, and sardines has led to a reduction in the traditional vegetable foods produced in Lacandon milpas. Although I am not a botanist, I estimate that of the forty-seven food plants commonly grown in the Lacandon milpa as listed by Nations and Nigh (1980:10), only two-thirds of these plants are regularly cultivated today.

With this background, I will now turn in the following chapters to the heart of this work, an examination of Lacandon religion and ritual.

CHAPTER FIVE

Ritual Objects and Sacred Places

The roots of Lacandon ritual behavior can be traced to the religious practices of the Prehispanic Maya Indians. Much of present-day Lacandon ritual is similar to the religious practices of the sixteenth-century Yucatecan Maya. The most obvious difference between the two sets of religious behaviors concerns the Lacandons' lack of elaborate ritual paraphernalia and the esoteric knowledge possessed by Yucatecan Maya priests in the Yucatán up to the time of the conquest.

Contemporary Lacandon rituals are materially simple and informal. The Lacandon do not have much ritual equipment, but those implements they possess correspond to ritual objects in use by the Maya before the Spanish conquest. Descriptions of these items are discussed and illustrated in the literary works of the time, such as the Popol Vuh or Landa's *Relación de las Cosas de Yucatán.* The use of some of these objects even dates back to the Classic Period (A.D. 250–950) and are depicted in Mayan codices and paintings from that time. Table 5.1 lists the principal implements used in Lacandon rituals discussed in detail below.

INEDIBLE RITUAL OFFERINGS

The Lacandon use a variety of ceremonial offerings that have a long history of use in Prehispanic Mayan religion (see Table 5.2). The most common offering is copal incense *(pom),* which is made from the resin of the pitch pine *(Pinus psuedostrobos).* Young boys are given the task of gathering the sap from the pine trees, which is collected by making shallow diagonal cuts in the trunk. The sap flows along the path of the cut and drips into a leaf cup placed at the base of the tree. The resin is then pounded into a thick paste and stored in large gourd bowls in the god house.

Pom is important because it is the principal foodstuff given to the gods. Although obviously not edible by humans, the Lacandon believe that when pom burns, the incense transforms into tortillas, which the gods consume (see Figure 5.1). On the other hand, the offerings listed in Table 5.3 are actual foodstuffs that the Lacandon feed to their incense burners.

TABLE 5.1 *Lacandon ritual implements*

IMPLEMENT	DESCRIPTION
Läk-il kʼuh	"God pot," an incense burner
Luuch	Balché drinking gourds
Xate	Palm leaf wand for feeding balché to god pots and for curing
Chäk huʼun	"Red paper" bark cloth dyed red and worn around the head during rituals or tied around god pots
Suhuy kʼakʼ	"Virgin fire," used to light incense offerings
Conch shell horn	Blown to summon the gods to the god house
Flute	Traditionally used to accompany ritual songs
Drum	Symbol of the Lacandon god Kayum, beaten to summon men to the god house
Meʼet	Wicker rings to hold drinking gourds full of balché upright
Xikal	Flat paddlelike board on which incense offerings are arranged
Balché chem	Dugout canoe in which balché is fermented
Pak	Large clay pot with the face of the god Bol on it and from which balché is served into drinking gourds
Kanche	Low stools on which ritual participants sit in the god house
Kʼikʼ	"Rubber" small humanoid figures molded from natural latex rubber that are burned in the god pots
Huyuʼ	Miniature wooden spoon that is used to feed the god pots

TABLE 5.2 *Inedible ritual offerings*

Pom	Copal incense
Chäk huʼun	Bark cloth headbands
Kʼuxu	Annatto, a red vegetable dye representing blood
Kʼikʼ	Miniature rubber human figures
Xate	Palm leaves used in curing rituals

FIGURE 5.1 *Burning incense in the god pots*

The Lacandon gods are believed to be fond of the color red and to enjoy the scent of *k'uxu,* a red dye made from the fruit of the annatto tree, *Bixa orellana.* According to Davis (1978:169), the red color is extracted from the fruit by soaking it in water to dissolve the red film around the seeds. This liquid is then dried to form a red paste that is mixed with white clay. When a man needs red paint, he grinds the clay patties to powder with a mano and metate and mixes it with water to form the paint. This paint is used to color a variety of objects, including beams in the god house, the ends of the *balché chem,* bark cloth head bands, ritual tunics, incense burners, the clay jar from which balché is served *(pak),* and even the faces of ritual participants, who may receive a red dot on their foreheads and chins and circles around their wrists and ankles. As discussed in Chapter Eight, this paint has symbolic importance, for it represents blood in Lacandon religious rituals.

According to Schele and Miller (1986), bark cloth was a valued tribute item and important in sacrificial rites during the Mayan Classic Period. During bloodletting rituals, strips of the bark cloth were pulled through earlobes and tied around the hair, wrists and ankles. The Lacandon today still use bark cloth headbands in their rituals. Called *chäk hu'un* ("red paper"), the headbands are made from the inner bark layer of the balsa tree *(Trema micanthra).* Long sheets of the bark are beaten against a small log with a grooved, round wooden mallet until the pieces are flattened and

TABLE 5.3 *Common ritual foodstuffs*

Balché	Mildly alcoholic beverage thought to be both physically and spiritually purifying
Nahwah	Tamales filled with either beans or meat
Säk ha²	"White water" atole, a cooked corn gruel
Käkäoh	"Cacao," a liquid chocolate drink

soft. The bark is then hung in the rafters of the god house until prepared for ritual use. The preparation of chäk hu²un first involves slicing bark sheets into long thin strips about one inch wide and twelve inches long. Once these strips are separated, decorative patterns in the form of notches and diamond shapes are cut into the bark strips to identify them as offerings to particular gods, while those worn by men are left·plain.

The chäk hu²un are colored red in the god house with k²uxu, the dye made from the annatto tree described above. This tint is mixed in a large clay pot filled with boiling water. When the dye is ready, the bark strips are added to the mixture in the pot, the container is removed from the fire and covered, and the strips are allowed to soak overnight. The following day, the red cloth bands are hung in the god house to dry. Significantly, these strips of bark that are dyed red with symbolic blood (annatto) and worn in Lacandon rituals were particularly associated with sacrificial victims in Classic Period Mayan art (Schele and Miller 1986:67).

As a ceremonial offering, chäk hu²un are tied around incense burners, the balché serving pot, and the southern end of the balché chem. After distribution to the gods, ceremonial participants tie their own headbands around their foreheads. At the ceremony's conclusion, headbands are left hanging in the god house but have no additional ritual use.

Palm leaves *(xate)* have a variety of ritual uses, but are most commonly used in curing ceremonies or folded into a spoon that is used to feed balché to incense burners. The Lacandon believe that sickness is a punishment sent by their gods when they feel neglected. Thus, when a family member is sick, the appropriate therapy is to go to your god house, burn incense offerings, and pray for a cure. As he prays, the supplicant passes a few palm leaves back and forth through the smoke of the burning incense offering until the leaves are blackened with soot. Then returning to his house, he sits next to the afflicted member of his family and prays while touching the sick individual with the blackened palm leaves. At the conclusion of the prayer, these leaves are stuck in the side of the house near the sick person's bed, thus leaving a marker by which the gods can locate the unfortunate individual and cure him or her.

Xate also have a frequent ceremonial use as utensils with which balché is fed to incense burners. In addition, the leaves are arranged on the ground as a bed for the pot holding balché during the balché ritual.

EDIBLE   RITUAL   OFFERINGS

Nahwah is a meat- or bean-filled tamale. Baskets of nahwah are arranged in front of the god pots as offerings, with small bits placed into the mouth of the figure molded on the god pot. After the gods have been fed in this fashion, the ritual participants then divide the nahwah among themselves. (As described in Chapter Eight, nahwah also has a symbolic sacrificial connotation.)

Säk ha², or atole, is another food offering. Atole is a corn gruel made from boiled corn sweetened with honey and which has the consistency of oatmeal. This, too, is fed to the god pots and then consumed by the men present in the god house.

A final offering is *käkäoh,* a frothy chocolate liquid made from cacao beans. As described by Davis (1978:213), the ritual sponsor's wife roasts the cacao beans and then grinds them with a mano and metate. While grinding the beans, she mixes in a grass called *aak²,* which makes the cacao liquid foam as she beats it with a grooved stick. Water is then stirred into the mixture and the liquid strained. The beverage is then poured into gourds containing balché or säk ha² and fed to the god pots.

I want to point out that these ceremonial foodstuffs are not prepared as dishes for everyday meals. Instead, they are cooked in the cooking huts built next to the god house using special kitchen implements. For example, grinding of corn and cacao beans is done with a mano and metate, not with the metal grinders found in every household's kitchen.

The offering and drinking of balché is a prerequisite for virtually any communal Lacandon ritual. The Lacandones believe that balché has a purifying effect and can help cure sickness, and therefore ritual inebriation is a common part of Lacandon ceremonial behavior. In general, drunkenness is not considered proper behavior, but because the gods enjoy getting drunk on balché, men are also free to indulge themselves during religious rites.

Only men are allowed in the god house to participate in these rites. In fact, there is only one ritual occasion on which Lacandon women are permitted in the god house (described later in Chapter Nine). Women's roles in Lacandon rituals are generally limited to preparing the ceremonial food offerings for the god pots and helping their drunken husbands home at the conclusion of a rite. Not surprisingly, present-day custom mirrors Prehispanic Mayan practice. Describing a sixteenth-century balché ceremony, Landa writes:

And they make wine of honey and water and the certain root of a tree which they cultivate for this purpose, by which the wine was made strong and stinking. . . . And after the repast the cupbearers . . . poured out drink from great tubs, until they [those celebrating the ritual] became as drunk as scimiters, and the women took it upon themselves to get their drunken husbands home (Tozzer 1978:92).

Although women are not allowed into the god house during rituals, they are not excluded from ceremonial events. It is common for women to watch the course of the rite from the cooking huts around the god house where ritual foodstuffs are prepared. Women join in the conversations, joking and gossiping, a part of any balché rite, and men bring drinking gourds of balché out of the god house to share with their wives and children.

Many early Spanish accounts speak of the Indian veneration of balché as a sacred purifying drink, and it brought great hardship to the Maya when the Spaniards outlawed its use. One Spanish source quoted in Roys (1931:216) writes:

Another reason why these Indians have diminished in number is . . . because they are prevented from making a wine which they are accustomed to make which they said, was healthful for them and which they called balché. . . . After they were drunk they vomited and were purged, which left them cleansed and hungry. . . . Some of the old men say that this was very good for them and cured them because it was like a good purge.

Similarly, the Lacandon describe balché as being physically and spiritually cleansing as well as having medicinal properties.

RITUAL TOOLS

The Lacandon use a variety of ritual instruments that date to prehispanic times. The most important of these items are incense burners, called god pots. The gifts of incense, balché (which is dealt with in greater detail in the next chapter), and ritual foodstuffs are presented to the Lacandon gods through the *läk-il k'uh* ("god pot"), a clay incense burner with the face of a god modeled on it. This form of god pot, with a figure molded around the bowl of the incense burner, dates back at least to the Mayan Classic Period, a fact exemplified by incense burners found in the ruins of sites such as Palenque. Evidence from Yucatán also illustrates that incense burners of this type were popular for household use by the Post–Classic Period (A.D. 950–1500). For example, personal incense burners with figures modeled on them were household items in the Yucatecan Maya city of Mayapan by A.D. 1200. The archeologist J. E. S. Thompson writes, "Mayapan's temples and shrines are strewn with fragments of large incense burners, of highly porous coarse pottery and up to eighteen inches high. Each had on its front, in relief the full length figure of a god painted after firing in brilliant color" (1966:147).

By the Spaniards' arrival in the early sixteenth century, the use of clay or wooden household idols was common throughout the Yucatán. The popularity and widespread use of incense burner idols are documented by descriptions of their use in several Spanish historical sources. For example, Bernal Diaz Del Castillo (famous as a chronicler of Cortes's conquest of the Aztec) was a member of the Córdoba expedition that discovered the Yucatán peninsula in 1517. In his account of the expedition, Diaz Del Castillo mentions seeing incense burner idols (such as those found at Mayapan) while exploring an Indian community (Wagner 1942:60). Similarly, Landa writes about the proliferation of these incense burner idols (Tozzer 1978:108).

The Lacandon center their ritual attention on the god pots because all offerings are transmitted to the gods through them. Each of these clay incense burners has an upturned face and is painted white with red dots and black stripes (Figure 5.2). God pots of male gods have vertical

FIGURE 5.2 *A Lacandon god pot*

stripes that represent the stripes on a Lacandon man's traditional robe, and female god pots are painted with crossing vertical and horizontal black lines.

The Lacandon have been called idolaters because of their use of god pots, which is incorrect because they do not worship the incense burners. The god pots are neither believed to be actual gods nor considered accurate representations of the gods. Instead, to the contrary, they are an abstract model of a human being, and the medium through which an offering is transmitted to the god for its consumption. In this sense, the Lacandon god pot serves a function similar to that described by Vogt (1970:13–14) for crosses among the Zinacantecan Maya in the highlands of Chiapas. Incense is burned in the god pots, and offerings of food and balché are literally fed to the image modeled on the god pot. Working with the Lacandon at the turn of the century, Tozzer witnessed these offerings and divided the ritual process into three steps. He wrote (1907:116–117):

> The article is brought in and 'placed' before the idols, or, as it is expressed in the chants, 'restored' to them . . . The gift is then offered to the braseros and their idols as a sacrifice, and the gods are asked to come in person and partake of the offering. Finally, the food and drink are 'administered' to the heads of the incense burners in behalf of the god. Posol [actually, atole] and baltse [balché] are placed on the mouths of the figures on the side of the bowls . . . whereas the offering of meat or buliwa [ceremonial tamale] is placed on the lip of the brasero with the fingers.

To Tozzer's observations I should add that not all of the gods are automatically given offerings. Before a ritual, gods are "asked" through *kinyah,* a divination, if they want to participate in the ceremony. Those that "answer" in the affirmative are incorporated into the ritual and given offerings. Those that answer "no" are simply left on their storage shelf along the rafters in the west side of the god house.

Adult men make and care for their own god pots, which are usually manufactured when an old god pot has been filled with the residue of burned copal incense. Younger men who do not yet have their own god pots use those of their elder male relatives. An owner of god pots can also pass his god pots on to his sons when he dies.

Formerly, new god pots were made every eight years in a month-long incense-burner renewal ceremony. Unfortunately, this ritual has not been held since 1970, and Robert Bruce's description of the ritual survives as the only account of the rite (Bruce and Perera 1982:29–31). In fact, it is a measure of the Lacandon's respect for Bruce that he has been, to my knowledge, the only non-Mayan witness *and participant* in this ritual. Noted mayanist A. M. Tozzer was not even allowed to witness this cere-mony when it was held during his fieldwork with the Lacandon at the turn of this century.

Although not thought to look like a god, the Lacandon god pot is conceived as a symbolic model of the human body. According to Davis (1978:73):

> When a god pot is made, it is crafted as a corporeal replica of the god to whom it is dedicated. Five cacao beans are placed in the bowl of a new god pot to represent the heart *(pishan)*, lungs *(sat'ot')*, liver *(tamen)*, stomach *(tsukir)*, and diaphragm *(bat)*. Specific features molded on the head of the god pots are the ears *(shikin)*, earrings *(woris u shikin)*, hair *(tsots'eho')*, jaw *(kämäch)*, eyebrows *(maktun)*, space between the eyebrows *(chi' u pam)*, eyes *(wich)*, cheeks *(puk)*, and mouth *(chi')*. The front of the god pot is called the chest *(sem)*, and the bottom is called the feet *(yok)*.

Furthermore, the god pots simulate, after a fashion, appropriate human ritual behaviors. Not only are they fed ceremonial food and drink but also the god pots are painted with red annatto dye in the places that correspond to locations where men paint themselves before a ritual: on the forehead, chin, chest, and feet.

When making or replacing a god pot, the most important object is not the incense burner itself but a small stone that is placed in the bottom of the god pot's bowl. These stones are taken from sacred sites believed to be the residence or temple of the god to whom the god pot is dedicated. For example, if a man wants to manufacture a god pot for the god Hachäkyum, he must make a pilgrimage to the ruins of Yaxchilan and take a small stone from the structure that is believed to be the home of Hachäkyum. This stone will then be placed in the new god pot. Davis (1978:74) says the Lacandon compare these stones to radios—"by means of these transmitters placed inside the god pots, a man's supplications . . . and offerings reach the gods in heaven." On the other hand, I have heard them described as *kanche,* the benches that the gods sit on when they arrive at the god house to partake of their offerings. Either way, the stones have tremendous ritual significance.

The Lacandon make god pots representing each of the major gods and their wives except the gods of the underworld, to whom offerings are not made. Only one other class of deities, the *chembel k'uh,* or minor gods, do not have god pots because they are considered merely assistants of the principal deities. The Lacandon believe that a major god, if he or she chooses to do so, can distribute part of an offering to their assistants themselves.

The use of balché and the offering of incense and special foodstuffs are not the only prehispanic ritual practices to survive in contemporary Lacandon religious behavior. Ritual purity was and still is necessary for participation in Mayan rituals. Both Prehispanic Mayan priests and contemporary Mayan ritual specialists such as *h-men, hi'loletik, to'ohils,* and so on must spend prescribed periods of time, lasting up to several months, in fasting, praying, and abstaining from sexual activity in order to achieve the level of ritual purity necessary to conduct their rites. For example, among the Lacandon, a balché ritual host is forbidden to have sexual relations between the time he makes balché and the conclusion of the balché ceremony. It is also expected that ritual participants wash their hands before entering or when exiting the god house. This practice ensures that one's hands will always be clean before handling ritual offerings or implements. This rule is particularly important for the host of a ceremony. If he doesn't wash his hands, his offerings will be impure and thus unacceptable to the gods. If the gods become angry, they may cause the ritual sponsor to become sick.

Ritual purity is also necessary for certain ritual implements. Another survivor of prehispanic ritual practice in Lacandon rites is the use of *suhuy k'ak'* or "virgin fire," meaning a new and unused fire. Landa, for instance, mentioned the use of virgin water (Tozzer 1978:144) and fire in sixteenth-century Mayan ritual. Describing the use of virgin fire, he wrote:

> Once having expelled the evil spirit, all began to pray with great devotion, and the Chacs kindled the *new fire* [my emphasis] and lighted the brazier for in the feasts which all joined in common they burned incense to the idol with new fire and the priest began to throw this incense into it (Tozzer 1978: 153).

In Lacandon rituals, when there is a ceremonial offering of incense, a virgin fire is kindled using a wooden drill kept in the god house specifically for this purpose. Sticks of kindling are placed in this fire and then used to light incense offerings placed in the god pots. Comparing this behavior with Landa's account above, one sees how closely contemporary Lacandon practice mirrors that of the Prehispanic Maya.

Although music no longer plays an important part in Lacandon rituals, rattles, conch shell trumpets, drums, and flutes are all manufactured by the Lacandon and occasionally have ceremonial use. For example, the conch shell may be blown to summon the gods to the god house in order that they receive their offerings of balché. The rattle may accompany certain prayers and ritual songs. The Lacandon also manufacture a combination drum and incense burner that is dedicated to the god Kayum, the Lacandon god of music. This drum was traditionally beaten ten times to summon men to the god house. Similarly, the Dresden Codex (Villacorta and Villacorta 1933) depicts priests playing flutes, drums, and rattles.

Even earlier evidence for the ritualized use of these instruments can be found in the murals at Bonampak. In room one, painted about A.D. 800, priests are depicted playing long horns, rattles, and drums made from turtle shells. The murals in room three also show men with horns and rattles.

TIME AND ASTRONOMY

The complex ritual calender and astronomical knowledge that governed so much of the life of the ancient Maya have not survived in contemporary Lacandon society. Instead, activities such as the burning and planting of milpas are timed by the blooming of specific seasonal jungle plants. Not all astronomical knowledge has been lost, however. The Lacandon still measure the passing of time by the phases of the moon. For example, two weeks would be expressed as *chumuk nah,* "half a moon." Seasons are usually expressed by reference to the *ya'ax k'in,* the term for year or spring, and the time of day is expressed by reference to the position of the sun relative to the horizon. Table 5.4 lists these terms.

The night sky in the Lacandon Jungle is an awesome sight. After stargazing in Najá, it is easy to understand why the ancient Maya were so interested in astronomy. Although stars in general are only referred to as *ba'al ka'an,* "things in the sky," the Lacandon name several stars and planets. As identified by Bruce (1974:107), they are: *kitam* ("the boar"), three stars in the constellation Orion; *Ah Tsab* ("the Rattle"), which we call the Pleiades; *Tunsel* ("the Carpenter Bird"), the star Rigel; *Chäk Tulix* (the "Red Dragonfly"), the star Betelgeuse; *Xaman Ek* ("North Star"), what we also call the North Star or Polaris; and *Ayim* (the "Alligator"), Ursa Minor. The Lacandon, according to Bruce, also recognize the dates of the summer and winter solstice.

The importance of Venus, deified in the cosmology of the ancient Maya, is reflected in the several names that the Lacandon use for different aspects of the planet. Some of the names found in Lacandon mythology are *Ah Sah*

TABLE 5.4 *Lacandon time referents*

NAME	TRANSLATION	MEANING
Hatska		Before dawn
Sasi	"To become clear"	Daybreak
Chumuk Chun K'in*	"Half base sun"	1–2 hours past sunrise
Ni Chun K'in	"Nose base sun"	Midmorning
K'ak' Chun K'in	"Fire base sun"	Noon
Ni Chun K'in	"Nose base sun"	Mid- to late afternoon
Mäna K'in	"No sun"	Sunset
Aakä	"Dark"	After sunset

*Chun K'in, "base sun," refers to the sun being positioned directly overhead.

Kab, "Star of the Morning"; *Ah Sah K²in,* "Star of the Afternoon"; *Nah Ek,* "Great Star"; *Kooch Ich,* "Big Eye"; and *Nah Xulaab,* "Great Destroyer" (Bruce 1974:107).

RITUAL PLACES

All balché rituals are held in the *yatoch k²uh* (god house), the thatch-roofed ritual hut. Set on the east side of the god house is the *balché chem,* a special dugout canoe in which balché is brewed. Although an observer may be misled by its mundane appearance, a god house is the site where secular space is transformed into a sacred precinct. The god house is built in a clearing apart from the village and serves as a ritual meeting site and a shelter for the storage of religious paraphernalia. Additionally, the god house is conceptualized as an imitation of the Lacandon gods' own houses. A Lacandon man may build a home with a cement-slab floor, board walls, and tin roof, but because the god house is literally the model of a god's house, it is always built in the style of the traditional Lacandon house—that is, with low thatched roof, dirt floor, and no walls (Figure 5.3). Red circular designs (a red circle with a solid red dot in the center) are painted on specific posts and beams inside the god house with the red dye k²uxu. These designs are a reminder of the time in the ancient past when the creator god Hachäkyum ("Our True Lord") sacrificed human beings, col-lected their blood in a gourd, and asked the god Ts²ibatnah ("Painter of Houses") to paint his dwelling red with human blood. Even the balché chem is patterned after the divine dwellings. It is covered with thatch when not in use (in essence, given a roof similar to that of the god house) and decorated with the same red circular designs as painted on the beams in the god house. Thus, when you approach the god house, you enter a sacred precinct. A god house is not simply a ritual hut, it is a meeting place between gods and humans, where they will sit in your presence, partake of your offerings, and listen to your prayers.

At the god house, ordinary reality is transformed into supernatural reality. It is the place where everyday items become sacred offerings. In the god house, the burning of incense transforms it into tortilla offerings for the gods to eat. The ceremonial tamale nahwah becomes human flesh, and the corn gruel called atole becomes "sacred water." In addition to food offerings, the incense boards *(xikals)* are used to symbolically craft human beings for sacrifice, rubber humanoid figures *(k²ik²)* are cere-monially given life and then burned as a sacrifice to the gods, and, finally, in the god house, the annatto dye k²uxu becomes a human blood offering. Even normal human speech is transfigured in the god house, becoming the nasalized singsong prayer voice used when speaking to the gods.

At Najá, the space in the god house is divided between the two oldest men of the community. During ritual activities, these two men sit in the

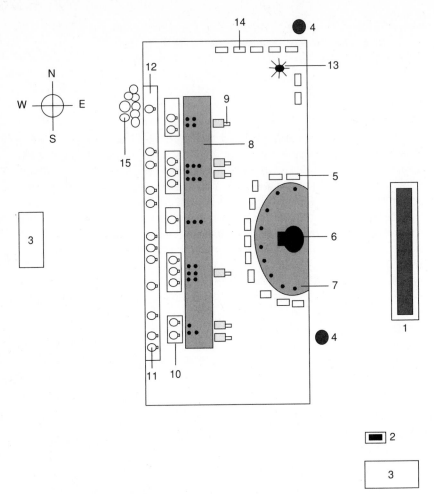

1. The *balché chem*, the dugout canoe in which the drink is made.
2. The *chem* for preparing *pom*.
3. The cooking huts where ritual food offerings are prepared.
4. Water bowls for washing one's hands before entering the god house.
5. The *kanche*, low wooden benches on which older ritual participants sit.
6. The Bol pot from which *balché* is served.
7. The *balché* drinking gourds.
8. Palm-leaf matting on which offerings to the god pots are arranged.
9. *Xikals*, flat boards on which rows of incense offerings are arranged.
10. Boards on which god pots receiving offerings are placed.
11. The god pots.
12. The shelf where god pots are stored when they are not in use.
13. *Suhuy kʼakʼ*, the "virgin fire" used to light incense offerings.
14. Seats for younger unmarried men.
15. Large gourd bowls used to store copal incense.

F I G U R E 5.3 *Diagram of a Lacandon god house*

middle of the assembled men, just as the highest status god pots are placed in the middle of the row of incense burners displayed on the floor of the god house. Seating of ritual participants is structured according to the age and kin relationship to these two elders based on patrilineal and affinal ties. In general, patrilineal ties supersede affinal ties. Between the two elders sit their first sons by their first wives. On the outer sides of the elders sit their other sons, ranked roughly by age, the oldest being closest to the center. Farther down the row are seated the sons-in-law of these elders. These seating rules are not absolute, but, in general, the individuals seated next to each other will reflect these principles of age and kinship.

The ruins of Yaxchilan, and to a lesser degree Palenque, also have religious significance to the Lacandon. The Lacandon make pilgrimages to the ruins at Yaxchilan (the Lacandon name for these ruins is *Chixokla*) to burn incense in the buildings thought to be homes of various Lacandon gods. At least since the turn of the century, Lacandon god pots and clay bowls of incense have been found abandoned among the buildings at this site. Although thought to have been the original home of the gods, there is no evidence that the Lacandon ever made pilgrimages to Palenque, be- cause, as one elderly man put it, "The gods are not there, they live at Yaxchilan." Palenque is said to have been built by the gods at the time the jungle and sky were created. Today, the religious significance of Palenque lies in the fact that Lacandon myths describe events said to have occurred at Palenque. In fact, many Lacandon men can walk among Palenque's ruins and describe the mythic events associated with each building.

One final class of ritually important sites are cave shrines (Figure 5.4). Although there are apparently several such sites, I have been allowed to visit only one that is situated in a rock overhang on the shore of Lake Itsanok'uh near the community of Mensäbäk. The shrine is dedicated to the gods Mensäbäk (the god of rain), Itsanok'uh (god of hail and lakes), and Känänk'ax (guardian of the forest).

The central focus of the shrine is a large incense burner totally obscured by a mound of burned copal that has covered the burner's figure. Scattered around this incense burner are hundreds of small god pots, clay bowls in a variety of styles, and three gourd bowls full of copal incense. Most interestingly, there are skeletal remains of at least four individuals in association with the god pots and bowls. Arranged on the ground between the piles of bowls and god pots are four skulls with the flattened forehead cranial deformation common to the Prehispanic Maya, one pelvis, four femurs, two humeri, one fibula, one tibia, and a small assortment of other unidentified bones. The Lacandon say the bones are the remains of gods who at one time took human form. When they returned to the sky they discarded these bodies. Although none of the material at the site has been dated, judging from the number of artifacts

FIGURE 5.4 *Human remains at a Lacandon cave shrine*

piled at the site it has been an important ritual place for a significant length
of time.

Also near this site are a series of cliff paintings. Approximately thirty to
fifty feet above the lake are a series of simple designs painted in red.
Although many designs are unrecognizable, several are clear and depict
outlines of hands, a monkey, and a couple of anthropomorphic figures.
Also pictured in black (described in Bruce 1968) is a more sophisticated
drawing of a serpent, jaws opened wide and swallowing some object.
When questioned as to who made the drawings, the Lacandon answer that
it was the god Ts'ibatnah, "Painter of Houses."

Thus, it is clear that the Lacandon not only possess a rich variety of significant ritual symbols but also that many of these items have been retained from the ceremonial practices of their prehispanic ancestors. Now it is time to take a more detailed look at the most common Lacandon communal ritual, the balché, and its importance in Lacandon society today.

CHAPTER SIX

🦋 The Lacandon Gods

The Lacandon worship a complex pantheon of deities of the sky, forest, and underworld, most of whom are directly related to the gods of the Prehispanic Maya. The supreme creator deity in Lacandon belief, the father of the gods, is named K'akoch. Although he is the creator of the earth and sun, he remains aloof, not caring about human affairs. He did, however, create the *bäk nikte'* *(Plumeria rubra)*, a flower from which the Lacandon gods were born. In essence, he is the same god as Xpiyacoc ("Twice Grandfather") of the Popol Vuh, and Hunab Ku, the supreme creator deity worshipped by the Yucatecan Maya (Bruce 1976:189).

The Lacandon believe the cosmos is multi-layered (see Figure 6.1), and although K'akoch is the creator of this universe, the Lacandon neither have a god pot representing him nor make offerings to him. Just as the gods created from the bäk nikte' watch over the Lacandon and depend on humans for offerings, K'akoch watches over the gods and they, in turn, make offerings to him. Thus, a pattern of mutual dependency between the Lacandon and their gods also exists between these gods and K'akoch (see Table 6.1). K'akoch's creation of the world and gods is described in a Lacandon mythic tale transcribed by Bruce (1974) and which I relate below. The verse numbers are those used by Bruce in his original transcription. The narrative is sparse and lacks detail in comparison to an American story because the myth is common knowledge in the Lacandon community. The narrator assumes that his audience knows the story's plot. The storyteller's role is to lead listeners through the account, structuring the narrative according to their comments and questions, rather than entertaining his audience with novel information. Items in brackets are my additions to the text; they make the narrative easier to follow.

CREATION OF THE EARTH

1 In the beginning was K'akoch, but not everyone worships him. The Lacandon do not know him.

2 Our Lord [Hachäkyum] knows K'akoch. K'akoch is his god.

3 K'akoch made the world, but the ground he made was not good. The earth was not hard.

4 There was no forest. There was no stone. He made only earth and water.

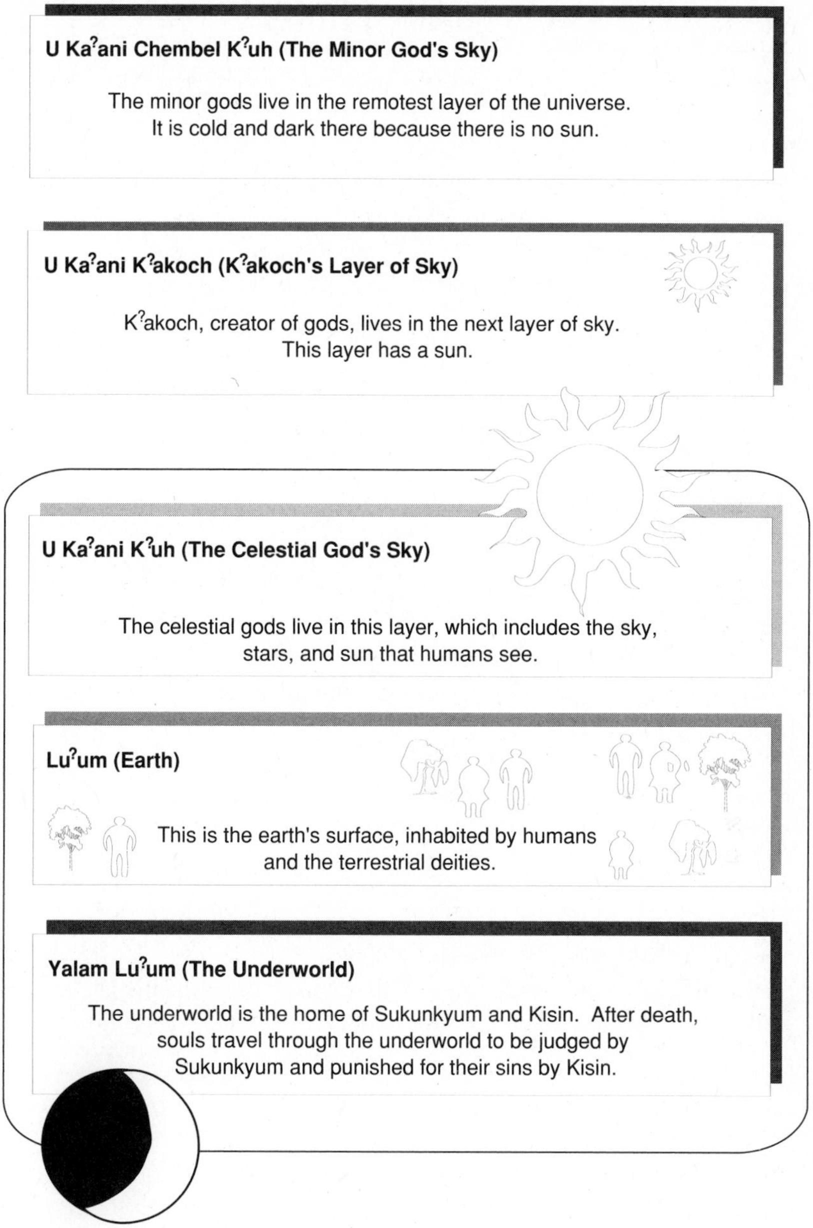

U Ka²ani Chembel K²uh (The Minor God's Sky)

The minor gods live in the remotest layer of the universe.
It is cold and dark there because there is no sun.

U Ka²ani K²akoch (K²akoch's Layer of Sky)

K²akoch, creator of gods, lives in the next layer of sky.
This layer has a sun.

U Ka²ani K²uh (The Celestial God's Sky)

The celestial gods live in this layer, which includes the sky,
stars, and sun that humans see.

Lu²um (Earth)

This is the earth's surface, inhabited by humans
and the terrestrial deities.

Yalam Lu²um (The Underworld)

The underworld is the home of Sukunkyum and Kisin. After death,
souls travel through the underworld to be judged by
Sukunkyum and punished for their sins by Kisin.

FIGURE 6.1 *Diagram of the Lacandon universe*

[5] Next he made the sun, and the moon for the sun.
[A common Maya belief is that *K²in,* "the sun," is male, while the moon,
called *Äkna²,* "Our Mother," is female. A Classic Period example of this

TABLE 6.1 *The principal Lacandon deities*

Äk²inchob	"Cross-eyed Lord"; god of milpa, son-in-law of Hachäkyum
Äkna²	"Our Mother," the moon goddess
Äkyantho²	God of foreigners and commerce
Chäk ik al	"Red Lord of Wind," assistant rain god, associated with hurricanes, the color red, and the east
Chäk xok	Miniature humanoid water beings
Hachäkyum	"Our True Lord," principal solar deity and creator of human beings
Hach Bilaan	Stone sculpture in ruins
Hahanak²uh	Hahanawinik, "Water House Gods," assistants to Mensäbäk
Itsanachaak	*See* Sukunkyum
Itzanal	Assistant to Hachäkyäm
Itsanok²uh	Lord of hail, lakes, and alligators
Ixchel	Daughter of Hachäkyum, wife of Äk²inchob, the goddess of pregnancy and childbirth
K²aak² Bäkel Äk Yum Chäk Xib	Hachäkyum's oldest son and older brother of T²uup
K²ak²	God of fire and war
Känänk²ax	"Guardian of Forest"
K²ayum	Lord of song and music

concept can be seen at the ruins of Yaxchilan, where depictions of mothers of rulers are sometimes set in moon signs, while the fathers are set in sun signs (Schele and Miller 1986).]

CREATION OF THE GODS

1 Now he [K²akoch] made the *bäk nikte²* flower. The older brother of our Lord [Sukunkyum] was the first born [from the flower].

2 Hachäkyum was born after Äkyantho².

3 When Hachäkyum lowered his feet [descended] to the earth he saw only the *bäk nikte²* flower. There was no forest. Hachäkyum said, "This is not very good."

4 Sukunkyum did not descend from where he sat on the *bäk nikte²*.

TABLE 6.1 *Continued*

Kebatun	Malignant, cave dwelling, female phantom
Kisin	"Lord of Death"
K'uk'ulcan	"Feathered Serpent," malevolent giant serpent, pet of Hachäkyum
K'ulel	Servant of Hachäkyum with Itsanal and Säkäpuk
ä h Lumkab	Minor earth deity, associated with rainbows
Mensäbäk	"Maker of Powder," Lord of rain
Nah Ts'ulu	Celestial jaguars, pets of Hachäkyum
Ot'uup, T'uup, T'uub	"Little One," youngest son of Hachäkyum and master of the sun
Paal Äk Yum Chäk Xib	Hachäkyum's second son and older brother of T'uup
Säkäpuk	"Hill of White Earth," assistant to Hachäkyum
Sukunkyum	"Elder Brother of Hachäkyum"; Lord of the Underworld
Ts'ibatnah	"Painter of Houses," lord of drawing, painting, and writing
Xka'le'ox	"She of the Sacred Breadnut Leaves," wife of Hachäkyum
Xtabay	Seductive nymph goddess
Yumbilil Ka'an	Hachäkyum
Yum Känän Säbäk	Mensäbäk
Yum K'ax	Minor forest gods

Äkyantho' did not descend either. But Hachäkyum wanted to descend to the earth very much.

5 Hachäkyum descended [to the earth] and stood erect. He went walking. He called to his older brother, "I am going to walk and see if the earth is good." Sukunkyum answered, "Good, little brother."

6 Sukunkyum descended with Äkyantho'. They left the *bäk nikte'* flower fully grown. As they passed they saw the land below the water [this phrase refers to Yaxchilan, the land below the Usumacinta River].

7 Hachäkyum first saw the houses there [the buildings at Yaxchilan] with Sukunkyum. Hachäkyum declared, "These are our houses."

8 Sukunkyum answered, "I do not know."

9 Hachäkyum said, "They are our houses; there are no people."

¹⁰ Later on, Hachäkyum saw Kʔakoch. Kʔakoch said to Hachäkyum, "Eh, this is your house." Hachäkyum answered, "Eh good Lord."

¹¹ Finishing their conversation, Kʔakoch left. He never showed himself again.

¹² There were three there on the earth. They talked among themselves. They said, "Eh, the earth is not firm, how can we make it hard?"

¹³ Hachäkyum said, "Wait, I am thinking." When it was almost midday Hachäkyum said, "I am going to go search for something to make the earth firm. Let's go." Sukunkyum answered, "Good."

¹⁴ There were small hills. Hachäkyum said, "Eh sand. First I will throw sand. He took sand and threw it over the earth saying, "Sand-sand, change it!" [And the earth became firm.]

¹⁵ Next Hachäkyum made the forest . . . he saw it was well made. As he watches, stone emerges, there is stone in the forest.

¹⁶ He finishes making the forest and all goes well. Now the earth is very good.

In this fashion, according to Lacandon mythology, the earth was made fit for life and the gods born from the bäk nikteʔ flower.

As described in the myth, Sukunkyum was the first god to be born in the flower. Thus, he is the older brother of Hachäkyum, and his name literally means "Older Brother of Our Lord." Sukunkyum is the chief lord of the underworld and the judge of souls. When a person dies, his soul must journey to the underworld, overcoming a series of obstacles on its way. Once in the underworld, he is judged by Sukunkyum. If he has led a good life, the soul is allowed to pass through the underworld and spend the afterlife in the house of Mensäbäk, the god of rain. If a soul has committed incest or murder, then Sukunkyum gives it to Kisin, the god of death, who tortures it with red hot irons and freezing water (this journey is described in Chapter Nine).

The notion of souls spending the afterlife with the god of rain, or in a watery place, seems to be common in Mesoamerican Indian religions. For example, the Aztec believed the souls of the dead stayed in Tlalocan, the realm of Tlaloc, the Aztec god of rain. Tlalocan is also depicted in the Teotihuatecan murals at Tepantitla, where Tlaloc is depicted with drops of water issuing from his hands as human figures frolic around him (Adams 1977). Water also seems to have been used as a pictorial metaphor for death and the passage through the underworld in Classic Period Mayan art. A good example of this artistic convention are the incised bones found in burial #116 at Tikal (Schele and Miller 1986:270–271). Given the symbolic link between water and death, it is not surprising that souls spend the afterlife with the god of rain, and a difficult river crossing is one feature of the Lacandon soul's journey to the underworld.

Sukunkyum is also guardian of the sun. According to Lacandon belief, as the sun travels through the sky, it expends its energy, becoming weaker and weaker until at sunset it descends into the underworld and dies. At night, Sukunkyum cares for the sun, feeding and carrying it through the underworld on his back from the west to the east. In this fashion, the sun is resurrected, strong and rested, and at sunrise once again begins its journey across the sky. As one might expect, during the day, Sukunkyum cares for the moon in a similar fashion.

Äkyantho' was also created in the bäk nikte' before Hachäkyum. Äkyantho' is the god of foreigners and commerce. The Lacandon say that he looks like a light-skinned foreigner wearing a hat and carrying a pistol just as do foreigners. He also is responsible for the existence of foreign objects such as medicine (the Lacandon traditionally treat sickness with incantations and prayers), hard liquor, cattle, horses, and disease.

Hachäkyum, "Our True Lord," is the principal Lacandon deity. He is the creator of the jungle, animals, and, with his wife's assistance, men and women. Although K'akoch created the original earth, Hachäkyum made it fit for life. Hachäkyum is also responsible for the creation of the underworld for his brother Sukunkyum. In this respect, Hachäkyum resembles the Yucatecan Maya god Itzamna, who is believed to be the Lord of Heaven and the son of Hunab Ku, the supreme creator deity in Yucatecan belief.

U Na'il Hachäkyum or Xka'le'ox ("She of the Breadnut Leaves") is the wife of Hachäkyum and co-creator of human beings. She and Hachäkyum also have three sons and one daughter. Their oldest son is K'aak' Bäkel äk Yum Chäk Xib ("Red Man K'aak' Meat of Our Lord"). The second son is Paal äk yum Chäk Xib ("Red Man Son of Our Lord"). These two gods are of minor importance, featured mainly as opponents of their youngest brother T'uup, who is master of the sun in Lacandon mythology. Because they sought to usurp their father's power, Hachäkyum's eldest two sons have been banished, forced to live in the forest without the honor given to other gods (Bruce 1967:97).

Ixchel is daughter of Hachäkyum, the wife of Äk'inchob, and the Lacandon goddess of childbirth. Identical to the prehispanic goddess of the same name, Ixchel is the patroness of pregnancy, medicine, weaving, and the moon. Unlike the Lacandon goddess, the prehispanic Ixchel had a sinister side in ancient Mayan belief. She apparently was also the goddess of floods and cloudbursts and was portrayed with crossbones, symbols of death, on her skirt. She is pictured in the Dresden Codex in this aspect (Figure 6.2), helping to destroy the world by flood.

Äk'inchob, the "Cross-" or "Squint-Eyed Lord," is the husband of Ixchel and Lacandon god of the milpa. He is believed to protect people from fevers and snakebite and, according to Baer and Baer (1952), helped his father-in-law, Hachäkyum, make the foundations of the earth and underworld with giant pillars of stone. As a deity of agriculture, Äk'inchob corresponds to the Prehispanic Mayan god the Young Lord of Maize, who

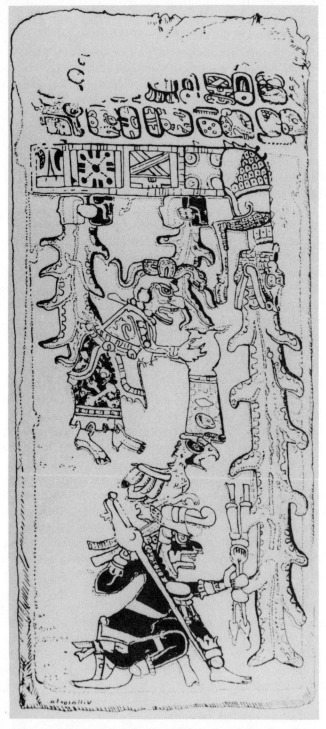

F I G U R E 6.2 *Ixchel and Itzamna (in reptilian form) flooding the world*

is pictured in the Dresden Codex as a youth with a maize headdress. Thompson (1972) believes that Äk²inchob may also be one aspect of the Prehispanic Mayan sun god Ah K²in or Kinich Ahau, who is often pictured with his pupils in the upper or lower corners of his eyes (thus the Lacandon "Cross-Eyed Lord" and his association with agriculture). Äk²inchob is also mentioned by Landa, who calls him Chi Chac Chob and says that he was one of the four idols placed in a temple and given offerings of incense, k²ik², and food so that these gods would protect the Indians' fields of maize.

ASSISTANTS TO HACHÄKYUM

Hachäkyum has a variety of assistants who help him carry out his duties. One of the most important is Itzanal, whose name appears to be derived from the Yucatecan god Itzamna. Itzanal's job is to guard the giant stone pillars in the underworld that support the surface of the earth.

In addition to Itzanal, Hachäkyum has five other assistants. First is Säkäpuk, "White Jaguar." The name *Säkapuk* is probably derived from the Yucatecan *Zacaal Puk,* who is mentioned in the *Chilam Balam of Chumayel,* a record of Prehispanic Mayan history and prophecies. In this manuscript, Zacaal Puk is described as one of the "four lineages from heaven, the substance of heaven, the moisture of heaven, the head chiefs, the rulers of the land. . . ." The mayanist Roys (1967:147) believes Zacaal Puk to be one of the early Mexican conquerors of the Yucatán in the Post–Classic Period and who was later deified in Mayan folk history.

Hachäkyum's next assistant is K²ulel, whose job is to sweep Hachäkyum's house (Bruce 1967:102). K²ulel's name is related to the Prehispanic Mayan title *Ah Kulel,* a class of authorities who were deputies of the *Batabs,* priests of the weather. Hachäkyum's fourth assistant is Bol, the Lacandon god of balché, whose features are modeled on the clay pot from which balché is served during Lacandon rituals. Bruce (1976:96) believes that his name derives from the Lacandon word *bolt-ik,* "to pay," and refers to the use of balché as a ritual payment to the gods. Another assistant, K²ayum, is the Lacandon god of music and song. In fact, his name means "Lord of Song." K²ayum is mentioned by Landa in a sixteenth-century account of a Mayan ritual (Tozzer 1978:106). Spelling the name "Cayom," Landa describes him as a ritual assistant to the Mayan priests. Similarly, in contemporary Lacandon belief, K²ayum is an assistant to Hachäkyum. It is K²ayum's features that are molded on the front of Lacandon drums.

Hachäkyum's last assistant is K²in, which means "sun." Although of great importance in Prehispanic Mayan religion (a pyramid at the site of Palenque was dedicated to the sun), K²in does not have any real significance in Lacandon mythology or ritual today. In fact, this deity is not the sun. Although the sun also is called K²in and is thought to be a supernatural being (but not a god), K'in the assistant to Hachäkyum and K'in the sun are different entities. Given the correspondence among the titles of Prehispanic Mayan religious officials and the assistants to Hachäkyum in contemporary Lacandon belief, it is not surprising to note that *Ah K'in* was also the title for "priest" in Prehispanic Mayan society.

One of the most important Lacandon deities is Mensäbäk, the god of rain. The name *Mensäbäk* means "Maker of Powder," which refers to the mythic process by which he is believed to create rain. In Lacandon belief, Mensäbäk makes a black powder that he gives to his assistants, the Hahanak'uh "Water House Gods." The Hahanak'uh, in turn, spread this powder through the clouds with macaw feather wands, making dark, rain-filled storm clouds. Mensäbäk is the Lacandon version of Yum Chac, the Prehispanic Mayan god of rain. Similar to the Christian Trinity, Yum Chac was conceived as having four aspects associated with both the cardinal directions and colors. The names and directional attributes of these four gods in one were:

Chak Xib Chac	"Red Chac"	East
Ek Xib Chac	"Black Chac"	West
Sac Xib Chac	"White Chac"	North
Kan Xib Chac	"Yellow Chac"	South

The Lacandon have retained and expanded on the prehispanic model of the Chacs. In current Lacandon belief, Mensäbäk has six assistants, who, like their Prehispanic Mayan counterparts, are associated with various directions. The Ha'hanahk'uh are:

Bulha'kilutalk'in	East (literally, "Flood waters from where the sun is seen to come")
Ch'ik'ink'uh	West ("God that eats the sun")
Xämän	North
Tseltsel Xämän	Northeast
Nohol	South
Tseltsel Nohol	Southeast

Once, while sitting in an informant's home waiting for a thunderstorm to end, I was told the Hahanak'uh are responsible for thunder and lightning. The god Kisin is said to insult the Hahanak'uh by raising his tunic (xikul) and exposing his buttocks to them. In anger, the Hahanak'uh throw stone ax heads at Kisin; upon striking the ground, they cause thunder and lightning. Lacandon hunters occasionally find these axe heads in the jungle, citing them as proof that this story is true.

Ak K'ak' ("Fire"), originally a god of war in Prehispanic Mayan belief, survives in Lacandon religion as the god who afflicts people with a variety of diseases, in particular, smallpox and measles, which are called *k'ak'* in the Lacandon language. This equation of disease with a god who was once the deity of war may stem from the Indians' realization that the incidence of several epidemic diseases correlated with the arrival of Spanish soldiers. Prehispanic representations of this god show him carrying a torch and a spear. The Lacandon label him as a carrier of disease because of the fever and red skin eruptions that are associated with afflictions such as smallpox and which they equate to being on fire.

Ts'ibatnah, "Painter of Houses," is the Lacandon god of art and writing. Although the Lacandon practice no distinctive art traditions aside from the decoration of their ritual implements, in their mythology it was Ts'ibatnah who Hachäkyum instructed to paint the gods' houses red with a paint made from human blood and annatto.

Itsanok'uh, "Great Alligator Lord," is the Lacandon god of hail and guardian of lakes and alligators. His name derives from *itsam,* an archaic word for alligator; *noh,* "great"; and *k'uh,* "god." As with that of Hachäkyum's assistant Itzanal, the name Itsanok'uh appears to be derived from the Prehispanic Mayan god Itzamna, the Great Alligator Lord of the Yucatecan Maya who was the Yucatecan creator god and deity of writing and painting. In the latter half of the eighth century, during the decline of Classic Period aristocratic culture, it appears that the belief complex surrounding Itzamna was subdivided into several separate deities that today are the Lacandon Itzanal, Itzanok'uh, and Ts'ibatnah. In effect, the Lacandon created a god for each of the attributes once held by the supreme god Itzamna.

Känänk'ax is a god of the forest. His name means "Guardian of the Forest," and the Lacandon say he protects them from jaguars and snakes. He is essentially the same god as the Yucatecan Mayan god Yum Kax, "Lord of the Forest."

The Lacandon also believe in a variety of minor supernatural beings. Some of these are the *Chäk Xok,* miniature humanoid beings who live in lakes; *Kebatun,* a malignant cave-dwelling female spirit; the *äh Lumkab,* an earth spirit associated with rainbows; and two commonly mentioned entities, the *Chembel K'uh,* "Minor Gods," and *Xtabay,* seductive female spirits of the forest. Lacandon mythology describes the Chembel K'uh as servants to the gods, and claims that they were born from the bäk nikte' flower after the major gods. Informants had little to add to that description, saying that the Chembel K'uh helped the gods but because they had no godpots, they were of no concern to humans.

The Xtabay, on the other hand, are better known. They are a type of female spirit who were purportedly created by Hachäkyum to service the sexual needs of the Chembel K'uh. But it is also said that the Xtabay may appear as beautiful women to men walking through the forest, seducing and then strangling them. The Xtabay are also a part of contemporary Yucatecan Maya folklore. Redfield (1962:122) describes them in the following manner:

> The Xtabai, well known in Maya folklore, is one of the most prominent of these demons of the bush. She appears in the form of a beautiful young woman, dressed in a fine huipil with fine embroidery (terno),

and with long hair. She induces a young man to follow her into the bush, or into some sascabera, and there, unless he is lucky enough to escape, she chokes him to death.

The Xtabay may be related to the goddess Ixtab of the Prehispanic Maya, although the function she served then is not clear. Based on her picture in the Dresden Codex and Landa's description, she is generally considered the patroness of suicides because her name means "She of the Cord," and she is pictured in the Dresden Codex as a woman who has been hanged by the neck. Thus, given the similarities of their names and the actions associated with each, there appears to be a strong connection between the goddess Ixtab, who is hanged by the neck, and the Xtabay, who strangle their victims by changing into snakes (cordlike objects). Thompson (1972:301) offers an alternative explanation for the depiction of Ixtab as a hanged woman. He believes that Ixtab is one aspect of the moon goddess, for the picture of the hanging woman appears in the eclipse tables of the Dresden Codex, and Thompson reasons that the figure refers to an eclipse of the moon. Although this theory is interesting, the Lacandon do not make any connection between the Xtabay and the moon to my knowledge. They do not even consider the moon a god.

Kisin is the god of death and earthquakes. As described in detail in Chapter Nine, Sukunkyum looks into the eyes of souls after death and judges their actions during their lives. If a person lied, was a thief, or committed murder or incest, his or her soul is given to Kisin, who punishes the spirit by alternate burning and freezing.

Although I have described male deities almost exclusively, the Lacandon also worship female gods. The Lacandon believe that the god's family structure is like their own, and that most male gods have wives and children. I have not described female deities in greater detail because, with the exception of those described here, the goddesses are said to mirror the actions of their spouses. Most goddesses are simply titled U Na'il, the "Wife of" a male god. When Hachäkyum created men, for example, U Na'il Hachäkyum ("The Wife of Hachäkyum") created women.

One final but interesting member of this group is Hesuklistos (Jesus Christ). Although not Christians, the Lacandon of Najá accept the divinity of Jesus Christ. The Lacandon resistance to Christian missionaries stems from their lack of interest in an individual whom they perceive as a minor god. Hachäkyum holds the place of paramount importance in Lacandon belief. The Lacandon accept Jesus Christ as a god of foreigners, and consequently believe him to be the son of Äkyantho', who is their god of foreign people and objects.

CHAPTER SEVEN

The Balché Ritual

THe following are field diary excerpts from my first trip to Najá.

July 14, 1980. Today is a balché drinking day and it appears it will be an all day affair. Only males are allowed. My first experience with balché was fairly simple. The ritual leader made an offering of balché to each of the god pots by placing a few drops on the mouth of the face on the god pot. He then placed stools in a semicircle around the pot of balché and invited everyone to sit down. The older men sat in these places forming an inner circle with younger men around them forming an outer ring. Not being sure what to do I sat outside the god house until I was invited in by Chan K'in Viejo. After that I sat with the young men.

With everyone seated the leader dished balché into drinking gourds and passed them out to the circle of men. Each man then dipped his finger into the bowl, shook his finger into the air (an offering?). Then it is considered good form to drain the cup dry in one draught. I drank only three bowls full, felt queasy and decided to quit. Balché tastes like very weak warm beer. Lacandon men drink bowl after bowl until they throw up, then begin drinking again. Mike Rees said balché cannot be stored or thrown out so drinking will continue until the dugout trough is dry.

5 P.M. The balché is finally gone. I am exhausted from sitting here trying to follow the conversations. With so many people talking at once I understand very little. One interesting thing: I saw several men's wives coming up to the god house to talk with the men drinking inside. I did not see any women drink balché, but Chan K'in Viejo said they could if they wanted to. I did see a man give his two daughters sips of balché from his drinking gourd.

July 16, 1980. Another balché ceremony is being held today. I walked by the god house at 6:30 this morning and it had already started. I know I should be down there but I just don't have the stomach to face drinking balché today. It is tough enough to face meals. I am really getting sick of beans, rice, and tortillas. I would kill for some chocolate right now. I am really getting depressed by the effort it takes to follow the conversations around me. All I want to do today is lie around in my hammock.

July 17, 1980. 7 A.M. God, they are having another balché ritual today, the third in four days. I asked why they were having them so often and the answers seem to revolve around two themes: 1) they are fun, and 2) people have a lot to thank the gods for right now. I suspect there is another reason—with the milpa work pretty well completed men do not have much to do right now. This balché appears to be more social than the first. The drinking is not as fast and serious and less balché is being offered to the gods. There is a lot of joking and fooling around going on in the god house.

11 A.M. A plane load of French tourists just flew in and they are wandering all over the village. I was hoping they wouldn't find the god house but here they are snapping away with their cameras while the Lacandon men continue their balché service. Now I know how zoo animals must feel.

The ritual use of the mildly alcoholic beverage balché was a common feature of religious life among the Maya Indians, according to early six-teenth-century Spanish historical sources. Because the balché rite involved offering the beverage to traditional pagan gods as well as ritual inebriation, missionaries soon attempted to terminate its practice. The Spaniards' strong disapproval is reflected in the following description of the rite, which was written in about 1566 by Diego de Landa, second bishop of the Yucatán (Tozzer 1978:92):

> And they make wine of honey and water and a certain root of a tree, which they cultivate for this purpose, by which the wine was made strong and stinking. . . . And after the repast the cupbearers, who were not accustomed to get drunk, poured out drink from great tubs, until they [those celebrating] had become as drunk as scimiters, and the women took it upon themselves to get their drunken husbands home.

Despite the long-standing prohibition against balché, today, almost five hundred years later, the beverage retains wide ritual usage among the Maya. In particular, the balché ritual is an essential part of Lacandon Maya ritual behavior.* Unlike rituals in many religions, Lacandon ceremonies are not differentiated much by form or ceremonial action. To the contrary, Lacandon rites are distinguished by the personal motivations or environ-mental conditions that necessitate the rituals. For example, one might hold a *ya'ahk'in* or *na'ahplil* ceremony as a thanksgiving rite to pay a god for curing a serious illness or for his assistance during the birth of a child. Or an individual might sponsor a *ts'a-ik u ho'ol* ritual to offer the first fruits of his fields to the gods. But whatever the motivation that prompts the ceremony, the structural framework of these rituals are the same and revolve around one central ritual element—the brewing and drinking of

---

*See Love (1984) for a detailed description of the use of balché in a Yucatecan Maya agricultural ceremony conducted in the community of Becanchen. Although not about balché per se, Love's article describes its brewing and use as an offering during the course of a Wahil Kol ritual held in April 1978.

the sacred beverage balché. In this sense, the balché ceremony is a *key ritual* (Ortner:1973) because it provides the ritual pattern around which almost all ceremonial interactions with the gods are organized. The balché ritual is also central to Lacandon religious belief because without the beverage, ritual interaction with the Lacandon gods would not be possible. Drinking balché confers the ritual purity necessary to participate in ceremonies where the gods are present in a godhouse. At the same time, intoxication on balché induces the trancendental state that allows men to have personal interactions with their deities, the foundation of Lacandon religious belief (see Appendix B about my film of the balché rite).

Drunk in large quantities, balché is believed to be both physically and spiritually purifying. Balché is used to achieve transcendental states during rituals as well as medicinally to treat disease. Together with pom (copal incense), balché is considered a favorite offering of the Lacandon gods who partake of this beverage through the medium of the läkil k'uh (god pot). In fact, the Lacandon believe their balché ritual mirrors a supernatural ceremony in which the gods make offerings to their creator and supreme deity, K'akoch.

Before presenting his gift, a man will pray, requesting a god to approach the god house (the ritual hut that is separate from the village), sit on his god pot, and partake of the offering that is about to be provided. Typically, incense offerings are burned in the bowl of the god pot, where they are believed to transform into wah (tortillas) for the deity to eat. Similarly, balché offerings are dripped into the mouth of the figure molded on the god pot. In this fashion, the gods eat and drink their offerings.

Balché ceremonies may be inspired by a variety of circumstances, but they are usually held when supplicants ask the gods for a favor in the face of serious misfortune such as sickness or crop failure (called *t'än-ik k'uh,* to "call the gods") or as a thanksgiving rite (*bo'ot-ik k'uh,* to "pay the gods") when they have granted a request. The Lacandon have no formal ritual leaders. Lacandon men are the spiritual caretakers of their families, and the relationship between these men and their gods is based on the fulfillment of mutual obligations. Lacandon men believe they must feed the gods balché, ceremonial foodstuffs, and burn incense in their god pots to ensure the benevolence of their deities. They believe that disease, death, poor harvests, and other misfortunes are sent by the gods if they feel neglected and become angry. Men therefore make balché for the gods when asking a favor or in thanksgiving rituals such as the *u ts'a-ik u bo'ol* (literally, to "give the head") ceremony, where balché and the first crops harvested from a field are offered to the gods. On the other hand, a man who has made the appropriate offerings fully expects the gods to fulfill their responsibilities to him and his family.

There is no ritual or calendrical schedule that decides when balché ceremonies must be held. Most are conducted out of a sense of spiritual necessity because they are directly connected to the physical and spiritual well-being of Lacandon men and their families. Because each man is responsible for his own family and close relatives, balché rites are held when an individual feels it is necessary. In my experience, these rituals are generally conducted every four to six weeks, but I have also participated in balché ceremonies held two days in a row and three times in one week. The linguist Robert Bruce speaks of participating in balché rituals on three consecutive days (personal communication).

MAKING BALCHÉ

Although several distinct stages are involved in the ceremony—making incense offerings, rounds of balché offerings, drinking by ritual participants, and so on—the order in which these events occur is not set and varies widely from ritual to ritual. Despite the variability of a balché rite's stages, the first step is always to brew balché in the early morning a day or two before the ceremony.

The man who sponsors the ritual, the host, prepares the drink with the help of one of his sons or a son-in-law. There are no secrets to making balché. Although a sacred drink, its recipe is common knowledge. First, the balché chem, turned upside down when not in use, is righted and filled with water carried in the *pak,* a large clay jar with the face of Bol, the Lacandon god of balché, modeled on it. Then a sweetener, usually honey but also sugar cane or even granulated sugar, is added to the water in the chem. Long strips of balché bark (the drink is named after the bark of the balché tree, *Lonchocarpus longistylus,* which gives the drink its distinctive flavor) are then laid lengthwise in the chem and held under the surface of the water with short wooden rods wedged into the sides of the dugout (Figure 7.1). Finally, the liquid is stirred, the top of the chem covered with palm and banana leaves so that rainwater and insects will not get into the balché, and the mixture is left to ferment the rest of the day and overnight. To decide which god pots will be used in the rite, the host conducts a short divination ceremony in which every god in the host's god house is asked if they want to participate in the next day's ceremony.*

CONDUCTING A BALCHÉ RITUAL

The ritual is usually held on the following day, although the host may let the drink ferment for a second day if he judges it too sweet. Around sunrise, the god pots for those gods who chose to participate are taken

*Although I have listened to Lacandon divinations, I was never allowed to watch them occur. Davis (1978:261) reports that the Lacandon practice three types of divination. The first involves connecting the tips of the fingernails together; the second, scratching the inner arm and watching for welts to develop; and the third (most commonly described to me) is accomplished by rolling a palm leaf around its stem and watching the pattern in which it unrolls. During each type of divination, the petitioner chants his question during the procedure.

FIGURE 7.1 *Making balché*

down from their storage shelf in the rafters of the west side of the god house and placed in a row on flat mahogany boards *(pätak che)* facing the east (the god pots always face the east, the direction of the rising sun).* The rite's beginning is signaled when the host blows several long blasts on a conch shell horn, calling the gods to the god house. Although men may come to the god house at any time, older men usually arrive there first to arrange the first rounds of balché offerings, which are placed in rows on a bed of palm or banana leaves in front of the god pots. Paraphrasing Bahr (1962), Vogt (1969:602) suggests that an area to be ritually purified has greenery spread on the floor. In the highlands of Chiapas, this is done with pine boughs, while palm leaves are used in the lowlands. In addition to the purification of the ritual area, the Lacandon believe the leaves protect the balché from contact with the earth, which would render it unfit for con-

---

*When asked why the god pots must face the east, Lacandon men answer simply that this is what their fathers taught them. Although not explicity stated by any of my informants, the ritual importance that Mayan peoples associate with the cardinal directions is well known. In this case, east is usually related with life, resurrection, heat, light, maleness, and strength; the west is conceptually linked to death, coolness, darkness, and femaleness.

sumption by their deities. Finally, a *suhuy k'ak'* (virgin fire) is kindled with a wooden drill to provide the embers used to light the offerings of incense placed in the bowls of the god pots.

The god pots are arranged according to the status of the gods they represent, which is similar to the principles that govern the seating arrangement of ritual participants. For example, Äk'inchob is thought to be an especially effective mediator between gods and men. Therefore, if the sponsor of the ritual is requesting that Äkyantho' (who sends diseases) cure a member of his family, then Äk'inchob may be placed in the center of the line of god pots (the highest status position) with Äkyantho''s god pot alongside. In other words, this placement of god pots reflects the host's desire for Äk'inchob to intercede with Äkyantho' on the host's behalf.

Incense offerings, *yo'och k'uh* ("god's food"), are usually burned first in a balché ceremony. The incense smoke's transformation into tortillas for the gods to eat is part of a larger principle of ritual transformations or reversals thought to occur during ceremonial events. Also, according to this belief, a small quantity of bitter balché changes into a large portion of sweet balché. Similarly, the palm leaves placed under the offerings become wooden seats for the gods to sit upon as they drink their balché, like the stools *(kanche)* utilized by ritual participants. Using *huyu* (small, wooden spoonlike paddles), a man places bits of incense into the bowl of the incense burner. He then lights the incense with an ember from the virgin fire, and prays squatting behind the god pot with the smoke and sparks of the burning incense billowing around him.

Lacandon prayers, structurally simple but metaphorically complex, are recited in a stylized, nasal, singsong chant. The content of these prayers are usually requests for aid, apologies for neglecting a god's welfare, and promises of future offerings should a god's aid be granted. For example, the following is part of an incense-offering prayer recorded during a balché ceremony in Najá. In this prayer, the recipient of the offering is Itsanok'uh, the Lacandon god of hail, lakes, and alligators. The man praying is paying Itsanok'uh incense for his future protection from misfortune, in particular from encounters with snakes and back pain. I have added the items in brackets to clarify the meaning of certain passages.

[1] Here [for] you, Itsanok'uh, here is your incense. Take it.

[2] The payment you speak of Lord of the Sky.

[3] Perhaps now your thoughts will not be cold to me.

[4] Do not allow snakes to emerge on my path when I return.

[5] If you, if perhaps you, Lord Itsanok'uh.

[6] Do not allow snakes to emerge on my path as I return to my house in Najá.

⁷ Here is your payment of copal incense, take it!

⁸ For you with my Lord.

⁹ Here for you the payment of copal incense.

¹⁰ Throw out [extend] your hands, you cure well.

¹¹ If there is pain in my back, [or] perhaps you see something bad I am sorry. . . .

¹² You see your incense burner.

¹³ Heal my back, you cure me.

[in lines 10–13, the praying individual is proposing a deal to Itsanok²uh. In essence, he says, "I am burning incense for you, so if I suffer from pain cure it. If I do something bad, then forgive me because I am making this offering.]

¹⁴ If you have seen me do something [bad] I am sorry, I am not guilty. . . .

¹⁵ Now I am not guilty . . . I have not slandered your incense burner.

¹⁶ I have not spoken badly about your god pot, I have given incense to you here. . . .

¹⁷ I am very happy to see your incense burner.

¹⁸ Here I have arrived to see it beneath your house.

¹⁹ It is good that I pay incense to you Lord . . . here is the payment of incense.

Next, before the men begin drinking balché, it is offered to the gods. Gourds of balché are poured from the Bol pot and placed in rows in front of the god pots. A *xate²*, a short wand made from a rolled palm leaf, is dipped into each of the offering gourds. A few drops of balché collected in this fashion from each gourd are shaken into a small gourd, and this balché is then fed to the god pots, literally dripped into the mouths of the figures modeled on the incense burners. In this manner, the gods drink balché as a supplicant prays that the gods accept his offering. The following prayer was recorded during a balché ritual as one individual fed his offering to a series of god pots, apologizing for possible transgressions, and asking the gods addressed in the prayer to heal a sick family member named Chan K²in.

¹ Here, Lord, here is your good sacred water [this term usually refers to atole].

² See this with my lord the wife of Äk²inchob [god of the milpa].

³ I am sorry if perhaps you hear things [you do not like].

⁴ I have not abandoned your god pot.

⁵ I am calling your god pot.

⁶ Perhaps if you have seen bad things, I am sorry.

⁷ Here it is, I give you balché.

⁸ Here you, Äk'inchob, here is your good sacred water.

⁹ Here you, Säkäpuk, here is your good sacred water. [*Säkäpuk* means "white hill." He is an assistant to Hachäkyum, the Lacandon creator god.]

¹⁰ Cure my uncle Chan K'in.

¹¹ You are the lord of this incense burner. Cure him [Chan K'in] of dizziness.

¹² Drink! He is dizzy, there is anger [or fever].

¹³ You saw that none of us drank balché without making proper offerings. . . .

¹⁴ His father, my uncle Chan K'in, did not drink balché without making offerings.

¹⁵ You tried it long ago [you previously sampled balché].

¹⁶ If you saw something [bad], my uncle Chan K'in is sorry, I am sorry.

¹⁷ With sacred water [balché], it can cure my uncle Chan K'in.

¹⁸ You see again balché offered here to you, Lord.

¹⁹ Here is sacred water for you. . . .

After the balché offerings have been given to the god pots, the host takes a second gourd full of balché, steps outside the god house, and offers a libation to all the gods in general by sprinkling the balché into the air with his palm-leaf wand, facing, each of the four cardinal directions in turn.

After this libation and prayer are concluded, the host of the ritual invites the assembled men to take a seat around the Bol pot, offering each a drinking gourd *(luuch)* full of balché that he has ladled from the Bol pot. When everyone has a gourd of balché sitting in front of them, the host addresses each man by a kinship term (only parents use given names with their children), saying for instance, "tech yum, tech mäm" ("you uncle, you brother-in-law"), to which each recipient replies, *"bay"* ("good"). Then the host invites those present to drink, everyone makes a small libation to the gods from their drinking gourd by dipping their finger into the gourd and flicking the liquid into the air, and balché drinking commences. From this point on, formal order of ceremonial events is abandoned. Rounds of balché and incense will be offered to the gods throughout the day. There is no set sequence of offerings; men pray, burn incense, and feed balché to the god pots when they feel like doing so. Some men may make no offerings at all, simply spending the day in the god house drinking balché, conversing with other men, and becoming pleasantly intoxicated.

It is the host's job to bring balché from the balché chem to the god house, serve the men attending the rite, and ensure that everyone keeps drinking, for the ceremony continues until the balché chem is empty. When all has finally been consumed (usually by late afternoon), the gourds of balché offerings set in front of the god pots are poured back into the pak and the men finish the last of the drink. With the balché gone, the Bol pot is put away, and the drinking gourds are rinsed and stored in net bags hanging from the rafters of the god house. Finally, the balché chem is turned upside down, and the host cleans up the god house, throwing away banana and palm leaf mats where balché offerings had rested in front of the god pots.

SOCIAL FUNCTIONS OF THE BALCHÉ RITE

Although the ceremony has a serious ritual purpose, it is not a solemn event. Men gather to joke, exchange news, and get drunk. Although recreational intoxication generally meets with community disapproval, it is considered a transcendental purifying state in the context of the balché rite. This attitude toward drunkenness in the course of a balché ceremony is neatly characterized by the following conversation between a Lacandon man and an American journalist (Bruce and Perera 1982:79):

> Chan K'in passes me a cigar and accompanies it with a little homily on smoking and drinking. "After you smoke a cigar you get dizzy and have to lie down," he says. "After you drink balché you are content and can still walk around. If you smoke a cigar and drink balché together, you are content and a little dizzy, and you can sit or walk around as you wish. It is perfection."
>
> Young Chan K'in adds pointedly, "And balché does not give you a headache and hangover like whiskey."
>
> I ask, "And what if you drink too much balché and smoke too many cigars?"
>
> "Ah then you get sick and vomit and piss all night until you pass out," Chan K'in replies. "The next day you feel like one newly born."

The balché is a very informal ritual. Men come and go as they please, stopping in the god house to drink balché, then leaving to eat, run errands, or go work in their milpas. After completing their business, men return to the god house and continue participating in the ritual. Although attendance at the ritual is not required, invariably every man old enough to drink balché (older than about thirteen) attends. Even boys not yet old enough to drink balché come to sit in the god house and watch and listen to the older men. In fact, small boys often sneak puffs off of discarded cigars and drain the dregs from unattended balché drinking cups in imitation of their fathers and older brothers. In this fashion, they learn the behavior and etiquette appropriate to the ceremony.

Men occasionally miss balché rituals if they are ill or gone from the village on the day of the ceremony. In these situations, balché is brought to one who is sick or saved for a man absent from the village. In Najá, of the twenty-four men old enough to drink balché, twenty-two habitually do so when provided the opportunity. Two men cannot drink for medical reasons; one has tuberculosis, the other is taking medication to prevent epileptic seizures. Although they do not drink balché, they still attend the ceremony, sitting in the god house and talking with the other men, thus participating in the social aspects of the ceremony.

Women are not allowed in the god house, and therefore do not participate in the mechanical aspects of the ritual such as making offerings and reciting prayers. Although prohibited from entering the ceremonial hut, women are not isolated from the ritual event. They often come to the god house clearing during a ceremony, sit in the ritual cooking huts, and talk and joke with their husbands inside the god house. It is quite common, for example, for a woman to call to her husband, "T-ah käla'an-ech?" ("Are you drunk?") To which her husband will reply, "Ne käla'an-en." ("I am *very* drunk.") The men, in turn, bring gourds full of balché out of the god house for their wives and daughters to drink. In effect, the balché ritual is an example of what A. F. C. Wallace termed a "rite of intensification." He writes (1966:30): "Just as nature requires ritual attention in order to assure that its fertility and benevolence shall not flag or fail, so the community of people from time to time needs to be restored in its attachment to the values and customs of its culture."

The balché ritual can be viewed as a means for reasserting faith in the traditional gods because the rite is primarily a ritual payment to these deities, followed by the communal distribution of balché. But the ceremony also serves as a stage for the performance of traditional songs and stories, and allowed to watch, children begin to learn about the balché rite at a young age.

After the ritual offerings of incense and balché have been made to the god pots, the men spend the rest of the day in the god house drinking and talking. The duration of a balché varies, for it lasts until the balché chem has been emptied of the beverage. During this final stage of the ritual, when men are drunk and the chem is almost dry, an observer is most likely to witness the singing of traditional Lacandon songs. Although Lacandon men enjoy music, they are usually reluctant to perform. But when men are fortified with balché, the rite can become a forum for the performance of songs covering a wide range of topics not usually sung in public. For example, the song for "when you are in the forest at night without a fire," and the Bol song (in honor of Bol, the Lacandon god of balché) are sung only during the balché rite.

One of the most interesting songs, "u K'ay-il ti' Box" ("Song to the Gourd") is named after the balché drinking gourds. This song is of particular interest because it contains several layers of symbolic meaning. On the surface, the song is a Lacandon "love" song, a man singing to a woman. The symbolic meaning of the song refers to balché. Lak Chan-eh, the "Little Woman," is actually a metaphor for the ritual drink. Finally, the song also alludes to the role the balché ritual plays in controlling deviant behavior. When the balché rite is conducted for this purpose, the song is called "The Liar's Song." Although I have analyzed a much longer version of this song elsewhere (McGee 1987), for the sake of brevity I will quote Bruce's (1976:39) translation of the same song.

THE SONG TO THE GOURD (OR LITTLE WIFE)

Once again I have wanted you, oh little woman. One of your measures.
Do not leave me, oh little woman.
Once again I have seen you, little woman.
Like ripe custard apples are your breasts, oh little woman.
Once again I have wanted you.
I will not leave you, oh little woman.
I feel completely undone, little woman.
Do not leave me, little woman.
My mind clears well, little woman.
Do not leave me, little woman.
Embrace me well, little woman.
Once again I have wanted you. Do not leave me, little woman.
Your breasts are custard apples. One of your measures, little woman.
Call me well, little woman.
My mind has cleared now, little woman.
Do not cast me down, oh little woman. One of your measures.
Once again I have wanted you.
Like ripe custard apples are you breasts, little woman.
I embrace you tightly, oh little woman.
Oh I will not leave you, little woman.

This song appears to be a love song to a woman, but it is actually about balché. The drink is personified as a "little woman," and the metaphor is followed throughout the song. The phrases "I feel completely undone, little woman," "Do not cast me down, little woman," and "I embrace you tightly, oh little woman," all refer to the song's metaphorical meaning and indicate that the singer is drunk. In general, the song is sung as a means of preventing vomiting after the singer has drunk a large quantity of balché and is feeling nauseated. Therefore, the phrase "Do not leave me little woman" actually refers to the singer's desire to avoid vomiting because it will cause him to lose the transcendental and purifying state of drunkenness that the beverage confers. The phrase "one of your measures," repeated throughout the song, refers to the gourd cup that is used to ladle balché into drinking gourds.

"The Song to the Gourd" is also called the "Liar's Song," which highlights the ritual's use as a mechanism for social control. In Lacandon society, the ceremony can be used as a form of public punishment. This use of the rite is sharply differentiated from the other occasions that inspire gifts of balché, namely, asking a favor of a god *(t'än-ik k'uh)* and payment to a god *(bo'ot-ik k'uh)*. Called *chun luch-t-ik* (to give the "base" of a drinking gourd), the rite is an occasion for the ritual punishment of minor transgressions, in particular, lying. The Lacandon conceive of lying as a form of illness. Balché taken in large doses is thought to cure illness as well as being physically and spiritually purifying. The drink also has a physical effect beyond inducing intoxication in that it acts as both an emetic and a purge. If someone behaves in a negative manner and ignores the remonstrations of his family or community elders, he may be subjected to the chun luch-t-ik. By being pressured into drinking balché until he vomits, the wrongdoer is punished for his misbehavior, purged of his illness, and spiritually cleansed.

Although a host's motives for holding the ceremony are different, the chun luch-t-ik rite is conducted in a manner that is virtually identical to a regular balché ritual. An individual who feels he has been wronged prepares the balché and arranges the god house in exactly the same fashion as he would a regular balché ritual, mentioning his ulterior motives to no one. Secretly, however, in his prayers before the ceremony, he asks the gods to make the wrongdoer vomit as punishment for the offense.

The ritual is conducted as usual, with men coming to the god house to participate. After everyone drinks their first round of balché, the offender is offered a second round and then one after another until he becomes thoroughly drunk. If this man refuses to drink, he will be openly accused of his transgression, subjected to teasing and criticism, and pressured to keep drinking. This hazing continues until the culprit vomits and is thus cured. If the suspect does not vomit, he is assumed to be innocent of the accusation.

Because of its diverse nature and multiple levels of symbolic expression, the balché ritual continues to be a viable medium of religious expression serving both the social and ritual needs of this Lacandon community. Characterized here as a key ritual, the ceremony forms the basic framework upon which virtually all Lacandon ritual action is structured. One ceremony can serve alternately as a form of ritual payment, vehicle for requesting a favor of the gods, or a form of ritualized punishment for deviant behavior. Furthermore, the communal nature of the ritual provides some measures of community cohesion because it is a forum for the performance of traditional songs and stories that reinforce the continuation and acceptance of traditional Lacandon lore. Finally, the balché ritual provides a nonviolent procedure for the correction of deviant behavior, a procedure that other Lacandon communities lack. The variety of social functions served by this ceremony are illustrated in the fact that the people of Najá continue to practice this traditional Mayan form of worship while its abandonment by other Lacandon communities has resulted in their conversion to Protestant Christianity. Although many details of the ancient Mayan balché ritual are not known, in contemporary Lacandon society it remains a multipurpose institution that continues to service both the religious and social needs of the people of Najá.

CHAPTER EIGHT

🪷 Sacrificial Symbolism in Lacandon Ritual

Symbolic representations of human sacrifice and ritual cannibalism are practiced in several forms in Lacandon rituals, principally during the nahwah ceremony. This rite is a variant of the balché ceremony, with the addition of nahwah offerings, ceremonial tamales usually filled with beans or meat. In the previous chapter, the balché rite was described as a key ritual because it serves as a structural prototype for virtually all Lacandon communal religious rituals. In addition, the site and implements used during the balché ritual provide a symbolic model for Lacandon cosmological and sacrificial beliefs. By their presence in the sacred precinct of the god house, the ritual implements and actions within this structure become symbols representing offerings to the gods. In the course of a ritual, these objects are transformed into sacred offerings. Outside the god house, copal incense is merely incense. Burned in a god pot, copal incense is transformed to food for the gods. The red dye k'uxu is used in a variety of everyday situations including as a spice in foods. But in the context of Lacandon ritual, k'uxu becomes human blood. In essence, the balché ritual and ceremonial offerings are a model for Lacandon cosmological beliefs. To understand the balché and sacrificial symbolism in Lacandon ceremonies is to take a giant step in comprehending the overall pattern of Lacandon religious beliefs and practices.

As shown in Table 8.1, the mundane elements of Lacandon religious life are merely models of their spiritual counterparts. The Lacandon god house represents the thatched roof homes of the gods, as does the balché chem when it is turned upside down and covered with thatch. As described in greater detail in this chapter, human flesh is symbolically represented by food offerings made from maize, and copal incense is transformed into tortillas for the Lacandon deities. Both human and animal sacrifice are represented by fashioning human and animal figures of k'ik', natural latex rubber, while the annatto dye k'uxu is used ritually to represent human blood. The red designs painted with k'uxu on the beams of the god house represent Hachäkyum's mythological decoration of his home with human blood. The Lacandon practice of painting red designs on their god pots symbolizes the prehispanic practice of painting their

TABLE 8.1 *Symbolic representations in Lacandon ritual*

OBJECT	SYMBOLIZES
God house	Homes of the gods
Balché chem	Homes of the gods
Food offerings of corn	Human flesh
K'uxu (annatto dye)	Human blood
K'uxu designs in god house	Decoration of gods' homes with blood
God pots	The human body
K'uxu designs on god pots	Painting of incense burners with blood and painting of ritual participants
Xikals (incense boards)	Human sacrifice
K'ik' (rubber figurines)	Human and animal sacrifice

incense burners with the blood of human sacrifices and imitates the designs that ritual participants paint on themselves before certain ceremonies.

Before describing the nahwah ritual and its symbolic elements of ritual cannibalism, I will begin this discussion by examining the various expressions of sacrificial symbolism in Lacandon ritual, including bloodletting and human sacrifice. In particular, Lacandon sacrificial symbolism can be understood by examining two "key symbols" (Ortner: 1973), the red annatto dye and ceremonial foodstuffs made of corn such as nahwah. K'uxu, the red dye, is significant because it represents human blood and is used to paint a variety of ceremonial implements, the god pots, and even ritual participants. Ritual foodstuffs made of corn represent human flesh. When ceremonial participants consume these foodstuffs, they quite consciously imitate the ritual sacrifice and cannibalism practiced by their prehispanic forbearers.

A variety of sources indicate that human sacrifice in a diversity of forms has been practiced throughout the Mayan area since the Classic Period (A.D. 250–950). Judging from evidence at sites such as Palenque and Bonampak, decapitation seems to have been the principal form of human sacrifice in the Classic Period. The more familiar practice of heart excision seems to have become popular during the Post–Classic Period (A.D. 950–1500) and is depicted in the Dresden Codex, Codex Tro-Cortesianus, and on a gold disk recovered from the sacred cenote at Chichen Itza (see Figure 8.1). To the horror of the Spanish, human sacrifice continued

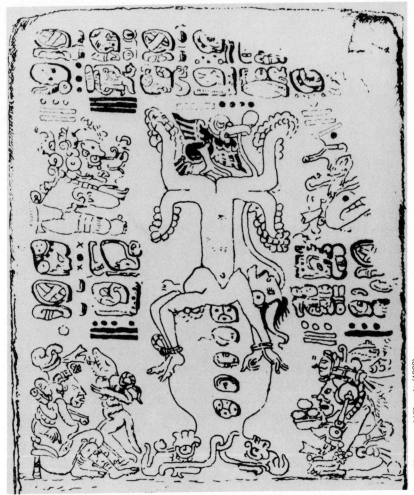

FIGURE 8.1 *Sacrificial scene from the Dresden Codex*

through the sixteenth and seventeenth centuries. Historical sources speak of Indians in the Lacandon area committing human sacrifice, with the last recorded sacrifice occurring in the highlands of Chiapas in 1868 (Soustelle 1984:3). Although contemporary Lacandon deny any knowledge of human sacrifice, their mythology contains references to the practice. In particular, the Lacandon have a myth describing an ancient people called the Nuki Nahwahto?. These people are said to have worn jaguar skins and sacrificed human beings to their gods by cutting open their chests with flint knives, feeding the victim's heart to god pots, and painting their god pots with the victim's blood. Obviously, this myth contains elements of historical fact. Compare the account from Lacandon folklore above with Landa's sixteenth-century description of the Maya's practice of human sacrifice (Tozzer 1978: 118–119):

> If the heart of the victim was to be taken out, they led him with a great show and company of people into the court of the temple, and having smeared him with blue and put on a coroza, they brought him up to the altar, which was the place of sacrifice, and after the priests and his officials had anointed the stone with a blue color, and by purifying the temple drove out the evil spirit, the Chacs seized the poor victim and placed him very quickly on his back upon that stone, and all four men held him by the legs and arms, so that they divided him in the middle. At this came the executioner, the Nacom, with a knife of stone, and struck him with great skill and cruelty a blow between the ribs of his left side under the nipple, and he at once plunged his hand in there and seized his heart like a raging tiger and snatched it out alive and, having placed it upon a plate he gave it to the priest, who went very quickly and anointed the faces of the idols with that fresh blood.

The similarities in the Lacandon myth and the historical account of sacrifice given above can be clearly seen. In both reports, the sacrificial victim has his heart removed, and the victim's blood is painted upon the "idols," the god pots.*

It is instructive to begin this examination of nahwah's role in Lacandon sacrificial symbolism with an analysis of these ancient mythic people called *Nuki Nahwahto'*. *Nuki* is derived from the Maya word *nukuch,* meaning "ancient" or "long ago." *Nahwahto'* is obviously related to the word *nahwah,* the ceremonial tamale used in contemporary Lacandon offerings. But *nahwah* is also a compound word, composed of the term *wah,* meaning "tortilla," and *nah,* which is conspicuously used in Maya mythology to denote "great," or something that possesses supernatural qualities. Two examples of this use of the word *nah* are *Nah Ek,* "great star," or the deified plant Venus; and *Nah Tsulu,* the celestial jaguars who will eventually destroy the world. Thus, nahwah is not just a ceremonial tamale. The term denotes a "great" or "supernatural" tamale, a substance that is food for the gods. Not surprisingly, because the Nahwahto' are those who fed the gods human flesh in Lacandon mythology, and nahwah tamales are fed to the gods today, contemporary Lacandon have conceptualized a symbolic link between human flesh and their ritual tamales. Not only the common derivation of the two words but also the actions associated with Nahwato' and nahwah reinforce this symbolic link. Nahwah is fed to the god pots, then divided for consumption among the ritual participants. Similarly, we know from descriptions by Landa and the Lacandon myth above that sacrificial victims had their hearts cut out and fed to the god pots; this was

---

*For other sixteenth-century accounts of human sacrifice in the Yucatán, see Robicsek and Hales (1984) and Wilkerson (1984).

followed by ritual cannibalism in which parts of the victim were consumed by the ritual leaders.*

Landa also speaks of the practice of anointing the faces of idols with a sacrificial victim's blood. Paralleling this ancient practice, the Lacandon dip their nahwah in a sauce colored red with k'uxu so that it resembles a bloody offering. Furthermore, as described in Chapter Five, k'uxu is used to paint ritual instruments, including the god pots. Red dots are placed on the forehead of the god pot between the eyes, the chin, the chest (the middle of the bowl below the face) and the feet (the base of the incense burner).

The Lacandon are explicit about the association between blood and k'uxu. Speaking of the Nuki Nahwahto', I was told that the god pots were painted with blood from the victim's heart exactly as contemporary Lacandon god pots are painted with k'uxu. The symbolic pattern thus appearing is one in which ritual food offerings are a substitute for human sacrifice, and annatto is quite consciously used as a substitute for human blood. Furthermore, this symbolic substitution of k'uxu for blood is fairly recent, because older men in the village all remember making ritual offerings of their own blood to their god pots. Lacandon men formerly cut their earlobes with flint blades, let their blood drip into the god pots, and then burned this blood mixed with incense as an offering in their god pots. This form of autosacrifice appears to have been discontinued in the late 1950s.

The Lacandon also sacrificed wild game as well as their own blood, offering the meat and blood to their gods with copal incense. This ritual behavior is also similar to Prehispanic Mayan forms of sacrifice. Landa, witnessing such a ritual offering in the mid-sixteenth century, described it in this manner:

> They offered the image bread made with the yolks of eggs and others made with the hearts of deer, and another made of dissolved pepper. There were many people who drew their blood, cutting their ears and anointed with the blood the stone of the god called Chac Acantun, which they had there . . . and meanwhile they burned their incense to it (Tozzer 1978:144).

The Lacandon believe that Hachäkyum and his wife made human beings from clay and kernels of maize. Maize, therefore, is the substance of human flesh as well as their staple foodstuff. Thus, in a symbolic sense, when feeding nahwah to the god pots and later eating it themselves, the Lacandon are consuming the substance of their own flesh in a form of ritual cannibalism. The symbolic transformation that occurs here is similar to the events that unfold in Christian communion, where a participant taking the communion wafer is said to consume the body of Jesus Christ.

---

*Landa, writing about human sacrifice says, "The custom was usually to bury in the court of the temple those whom they had sacrificed, or else they ate them, dividing them up among those who had arrived." (Tozzer, 1978:87).

In addition, the use of the color red as symbolic blood is common in Lacandon ritual. The Lacandon believe red is a favorite color of the gods because it is associated with blood. Bark cloth headbands are dyed red for ceremonial use. Red circular designs are painted in the god house, the balché chem, the Bol pot from which balché is served, and the god pots. It was also common for Lacandon men to paint themselves red for ritual purposes. Although I have only seen photographs of this action, both Tozzer (1907) and Davis (1978) describe Lacandon men painting red spots on their foreheads and chins, as well as lines circling their ankles and wrists, a pattern which corresponds to the ritual decoration of the god pots with red dots.

It is also possible that this ritual body painting is done in imitation of the common Prehispanic Maya practice of ritual bloodletting. This bloodletting was generally accomplished by cutting one's ears or piercing the tongue or penis with a cactus or stingray spine. Describing this practice in the sixteenth-century, Landa wrote:

> They offered sacrifices of their own blood, sometimes cutting themselves around in pieces. . . . Other times they pierced their cheeks, at others their lower lips . . . at others they pierced their tongues in a slanting direction from side to side and passed bits of straw through the holes.[*]

Graphic representations of ritual bloodletting can be found in a variety of Classic Period archeological sites familiar to the Lacandon, in particular Bonampak and Yaxchilan. One section of the murals at the ruins of Bonampak (which, judging from long count dates found at the site, were painted around A.D. 800) depicts women sitting on a raised platform and making offerings of their own blood by piercing their tongues. One woman is caught in the act, poised over a bowl of paper into which she drips her blood. Presumably, the paper was then burned with incense as an offering. Standing below her is an attendant handing her a sharp blade. From Yaxchilan is the famous lintel 24, which depicts a bloodletting rite conducted on October 28, 709 (see Figure 8.2). This lintel portrays Lady Xoc, wife of Shield Jaguar king of Yaxchilan, drawing a thorn-lined cord through her tongue during a bloodletting ceremony (Schele and Miller, 1986). Dotted scrolls on her lips and cheeks represent the blood she has shed.[†]

There are also references to blood in Lacandon myths. In one myth, for example, the god Hachäkyum gathers his people together, cuts their throats, and collects the blood in a gourd, mixing it with k'uxu. He then gives this mixture to the god Ts'ibatnah (Painter of Houses) and instructs

---

[*]Tozzer, 1978:113.
[†]A particularly thorough discussion of Classic Period Mayan bloodletting practices can be found in Schele and Miller's (1986) exquisite work on Maya art and iconography, *The Blood of Kings.*

FIGURE 8.2 *Lintel 24 from Yaxchilan: Lady Xoc makes an offering of blood by drawing a thorned cord through her tongue*

him to paint the gods' houses red. Therefore, the designs painted in the god house and balché chem with annatto imitate the mythological event in which designs were painted in human blood on the gods' homes.

Another form of Lacandon ritual offering, k'ik', links the symbolic human sacrifice in Lacandon rituals with the ceremonial use of annatto as blood. K'ik', humanoid figures made of natural rubber, are burned in the god pots with incense. K'ik' seem to have been in general use by the Prehispanic Maya as a ritual offering. Landa mentions the burning of k'ik' as an offering to the gods, and at Chichen Itza rubber figures were thrown into the sacred cenote as offerings (Thompson 1954:114). The Spaniards also noted the use of *k'ik'* in the Lacandon's area soon after the conquest. For example, Thompson (1952:193) discusses reports from an entrada into the lowlands of Chiapas in 1586 that describes the discovery of wax and rubber idols.

Bruce (1973) describes the two types of k'ik' generally used in Lacandon rituals that are made from the sap of the rubber tree *(Castilla elastica)* (see Figure 8.3). The first is *täka'an u nok' k'ik'* or "k'ik' with clothes." These figures, as tall as twenty centimeters, are considered male and created in an anatomically realistic fashion to the point of having genitals. The second type, *tulis k'ik',* are much smaller, being only five to eight centimeters tall. These figures are made in a stylized triangular form and can be either male or female. Female tulis k'ik' are called *chel,* a reference to the ancient Maya goodess *Ixchel* (the moon). The male figures are called *k'ohol,* but the name does not appear to refer to any other object.

K'ik' are burned in the god pots with incense. The Lacandon believe that after burning, these objects become attendants to the gods, washing their deities' hands and mouths, lighting their cigars, working in the gods' fields, and making offerings to the supreme deity K'akoch for the well-being of their masters. This belief reflects the human sacrificial nature of the event, because the ancient Maya believed sacrificial victims were conveyed directly to the gods, becoming servants and messengers. The sacrificial symbolism of the act is reinforced by the fact that Lacandon worshippers formerly painted the figures with their own blood before burning them in order to make the offering more pleasing to the gods. According to Davis (1978:158), each man would collect his blood in a palm leaf and then paint his rubber figures. This was often done during balché ceremonies. Consequently, ritual intoxication on the beverage would lessen the pain suffered by men making blood offerings.

Today, as bloodletting is no longer practiced, the figures are painted red with the symbolic blood k'uxu. It is also interesting to note that the word *k'ik'* is the root of the Maya word for blood *(k'ik'el),* which further strengthens the symbolic connection between k'ik', k'uxu, human blood, and symbolic sacrifice.

Once the incense figures are molded and ready to burn, a special chant is recited over them to bring the figures to life. This chant, reproduced below, was recorded by Davis (1978:137–140).

My foot is afraid. My hand is afraid. Awaken. I awaken them and they stand on the board. I, I formed their livers, I, I formed their bones, I, I formed their lungs. I, I formed their hearts. I awaken them, and they

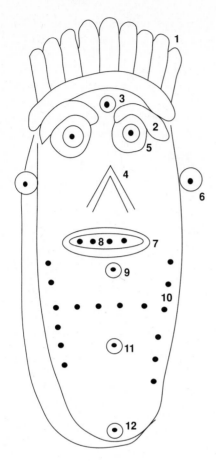

1. hair (*tsotel u ho$^?$ol*)
2. eyebrows (*maktun*)
3. nasal mucous (*u kapir u ni$^?$*)
4. nose (*ni$^?$*)
5. eyes (*wich*)
6. ears (*xikin*)
7. mouth (*chi$^?$*)
8. teeth (*koh*)
9. navel (*tuuch*)
10. arm hair (*tsotsel in k$^?$äp*)
11. penis (*chur*)
12. anus (*wit*)

Source: Davis 1978: 133.

FIGURE 8.3 *Parts of the rubber figure offerings*

come and stand on the board. They are for you from me Yumbilika'an [Lord of the Sky, another name for Hachäkyum]. They are for you from me, Ak'inchob. They are for you from me, Mensäbäk. They are for you from me, Itsanok'uh. They are for you from me Äkyantho'. For all the gods. I set them down, and they come and stand on the board. The rubber figures. These very rubber figures. They are near their feather crowns. They are near their (god pot's) heads. All of these copal lumps. I hold them up and they come and stand on the board. I, I truly awaken them. These *hirih* beams are your house, and I am your father. Here is your house, and I am your mother. The *chäk op* wood, this *chäk op* wood, this the *hirih* beam of your house, and I am your father. This is the *hirih* beam of your house, and I am your mother. The *chäk op* beams. The palmetto leaves are your house (roof), and I am your father. The *xa'an* palm leaves are your house (roof), and I am your mother.

This is your house, and I am your father. I awaken them, and they stand on the board. I set them down, and I hold them high for you, for you to accept, Lords. The na'ahplil ceremony is for you from me. The ya'ahk'in ceremony is for you from me. The witsbir ceremony is for you from me. I awaken you. They come and stand on the board. The tikinwah ceremony is for you from me. I hold these up, and they come and stand on the board. Ah, the fly is on the tikinwah tamales. There is also corn drink for the Lords. I awaken them, and they stand on the board . . .

In this fashion, the k'ik' are awakened and sacrificed to the gods as they are burned with incense in the god pots.

As stated above, the name *k'ik'* derives from the Maya word for blood, *k'ik'el*. A mythic association between these terms is found in the Popol Vuh, the mythological history of the Quiche Maya people, in a story about the maiden Xquic, "Lady Blood" (or Xkik; *x* is a feminine prefix in the Maya language) and her father Cuchumaquic ("To Carry Blood" or "Blood Carrier").

In the story, two mythic hero brothers (Hun-hunahpu and Vucub-Hunahpu) are challenged to undergo a series of trials by the Lords of Xibalba, which is the underworld in Quiche mythology. Failing in the last test, the brothers are sacrificed. Before burying the bodies, the Lords of Xibalba cut off the head of Hun-hunahpu and hanged it in a tree by the road. Instantly, the tree was filled with fruit, although it had never before been productive. In wonder at this event, the Lords of Xibalba decreed that no one should pick fruit from this tree.

Cuchumaquic told his daughter Xquic about the tree, and she decided to go see this wonder for herself. Upon her arrival at the tree, the head of Hun-hunahpu told Xquic that the fruit she saw were only skulls, but that if she would like one of them she should reach out her hand. Xquic reached up, the skull spat into her hand, and in this fashion Xquic was impregnated.

Six months later, Cuchumaquic noticed that his daughter was pregnant and demanded to know who was responsible for her pregnancy. Xquic answered before an assembled council of Lords that there was no father, she was still a virgin. Judging her to be lying, and believing that he had been dishonored, Cuchumaquic ordered that his daughter be sacrificed and commanded four of his messengers to cut out her heart and bring it back in a gourd. The girl, not wishing to die, concocted a plan to fool the lords of the underworld. Leading the messengers to a tree, she said (Recinos 1978:122–123):

Neither shall my heart be burned before them. Gather the product of this tree," said the maiden. The red sap gushing forth from the tree fell in the gourd and with it they made a ball which glistened and took the shape of a heart. The tree gave forth sap similar to blood, with the appearance of real blood. Then the blood, or that is to say the sap of the red tree, clotted and formed a very bright coating inside the gourd, like clotted blood; meanwhile the tree glowed at the work of the maiden.

Finishing their work, the girl slipped away and the messengers returned with the gourd of sap. The final passages of the chapter provide a description of how the lords of the underworld received this offering. Notice, too, that the mythological passage also describes contemporary Lacandon ritual use of k'ik', where an offering (in this case, a human heart) is fashioned from the sap of a tree and burned as a gift to the gods.

> When they arrived in the presence of the Lords, all were waiting. "You have finished?" asked Hun-Came. "All is finished my Lords. Here in the bottom of the gourd is the heart." "Very well. Let us see," exclaimed Hun-Came. And grasping it with his fingers he raised it, the shell broke and the blood flowed bright red in color. "Stir up the fire and put it on the coals," said Hun-Came. As soon as they threw it on the fire, the men of Xibalba began to sniff and drawing near to it, they found the fragrance of the heart very sweet.

Just as the Lords of Xibalba gather to sniff the sweet scent of the burning offering (a human heart manufactured from tree sap) in the Quiche Maya myth, so too the Lacandon gods are believed to come to the god house to partake of humanoid rubber figures (manufactured from tree sap), which have been painted red with the symbolic blood k'uxu.

After k'ik', the final form of sacrificial symbolism in Lacandon ritual are *xikals,* paddlelike boards about one foot square, upon which are placed rows of copal incense nodules or *tulis k'ik'.* When a Lacandon man prepares a xikal, the rows of incense are imagined to be male and female, with each individual incense nodule representing a part of the human body. For example, as he places bits of copal in rows upon the xikal, he might say, "This is your head, this is your head. This is your arm, this is your arm." In this manner, symbolic human beings are patterned out of incense on the board. When the xikal has been completed and the gods have been asked to accept the offering, the incense is removed from the board's surface and burned in a god pot. Similar to the k'ik', the xikal offerings are thought to be transformed into living servants to the gods as they are burned.

As with other elements of Lacandon ceremonies, xikals appear to have been a part of Prehispanic Maya ritual. Bishop de Landa described their use in the sixteenth-century Yucatán. He writes (Tozzer 1978:152):

> It was at this time that they chose officials, the Chacs, to assist the priest, and he prepared a large number of little balls of fresh incense upon little boards which the priests had for this purpose, so that the fasters and abstainers ["fasters and abstainers" refers to ritual participants who had been maintaining ritual purity through fasting and sexual abstinence] might burn them in honor of their idols.

THE NAHWAH CEREMONY

Having discussed the forms that Lacandon sacrificial symbolism take, I will now discuss one ritual in which symbolic human cannibalism occurs, the nahwah ceremony. Preparation for a nahwah rite begins two days before the actual ceremony when the ritual sponsor's wife cooks the nahwah. The tamales are prepared in one of two kitchen huts next to the god house where ritual food offerings must be cooked. The corn shells for the nahwah are made by grinding the corn by hand with a mano and metate. Filling for the tamales, usually black beans, is cooked in a large clay pot over an open fire and folded into the corn shell. The completed tamales are then wrapped in banana leaves, baked, and stored in large wicker baskets.

In the nahwah rites in which I participated, balché was mixed by the ritual hosts the day before the ceremony and left to ferment overnight. These hosts then spent the rest of the day in the god house, praying for the gods to accept their offerings and burning incense, not stopping even to take meals. During breaks from their prayers, the hosts prepared xikals for the following day's ritual (Figure 8.4). This behavior is reminiscent of the Prehispanic Mayan procedure for establishing ritual purity. Before an important ceremony, Mayan priests might spend weeks in fasting and prayer. The Lacandon ritual sponsors also "bathed" themselves in the smoke of the burning incense by dipping their hands into the flame and

FIGURE 8.4 *Preparation of a xikal*

smoke and waving the smoke over themselves as if splashing water on their faces. Similarly, "washing" in smoke was a common method of ritual purification among many aboriginal American peoples.

Nahwah rituals begin at sunrise. God pots of those gods who have "chosen" to participate in the ritual are placed facing east on a bed of palm leaves that has been prepared for them. As participants arrive at the god house, the ceremonial hosts invite them to sit down and administer the first round of balché offerings to the god pots. A host places gourds of balché along with baskets of nahwah and xikals of incense in front of each of the god pots, and balché is fed to all of the god pots with the xate[?] (palm leaves), exactly as in a balché ritual. A prayer and libation of balché is sprinkled in the air to the four cardinal directions as an offering to the gods of the forest, and participants begin drinking.

Soon after drinking commences, a virgin fire is kindled and one of the ritual's sponsors steps out of the god house to offer another set of prayers and libations to the gods of the forest (spraying the balché to the four directions). Reentering the god house, he lights offerings of incense in the god pots while others feed the incense burners more balché. As with the balché ceremony, the atmosphere in the god house is informal. While one of the hosts makes offerings to the gods, other participants continue to talk and drink balché, choosing to make their personal balché offerings at their own initiative. Rounds of offerings, prayers, and balché drinking continue unabated until the late afternoon.

When the balché has been finished, small pots of beans cooked in a bright red sauce (made from annatto, the same coloring used for the bark cloth headbands) are brought to the god house and placed with the baskets of nahwah as offerings in front of the god pots. In groups of two and three, every one of the ritual participants then picks up a pot of beans in each hand and stands for a moment in front of the god pots in prayer. This is the only rite during which I witnessed groups of Lacandon men praying in concert. In other rituals, men simply recited their own independent prayers at the same time. At the conclusion of these prayers, the ritual hosts tear a small opening in each of the banana leaf packets containing nahwah. Taking a bit of the tamale in their left hands, they dip their right hands into the pot of beans, and drip the red sauce onto the nahwah. This piece of tamale dripping with red sauce is then placed in the mouth of the face on the god pot accompanied by the following prayer.* Items in brackets are my additions to the text.

[1] Here it is, Lord Mensäbäk.

[2] Ts²ibatnah here. See it then.

[3] Very close he passes, he walks Säkapuk-eh.

---

*This prayer for the offering of nahwah was recorded by linguist Robert Bruce (1974:320–326)

⁴ See your food tortillas [tamales]. See where they, the grove of palms, are. [Refers to the bed of palm leaves on which the offerings are placed.]

⁵ See [the offerings], with sil [small god pots for the assistants to the gods]. See it then, the payment [for our] welfare.

⁶ You took them there, you go to Itsanok'uh. You enter there.

⁷ Here goes one [nahwah], Itsanok'uh. One you take.

⁸ You take one, here my mother.

⁹ You go to the Lord of the Sky. Here, go and give it.

¹⁰ We see him go from the grove of palms. It is clear. We will not be careless. . . .

¹⁶ See it, mother, see it. His older brother, my Lord.

¹⁷ Look Xk'anle'ox-eh [Hachäkyum's wife]. Ki Chak Chob [Ak'inchob], see the sikil-wah [tamales with gourd seed] for the Lord of the Sky.

¹⁸ It is good they make my sacred water [atole]. It is good my food [my wife, she who makes my food is well]. My sons are well.

¹⁹ My sons are all gathered together, all gathered together. It is good, Lord.

²⁰ All together [with] me. I am with my [son] K'in. I am with my son Chan K'in. We are all together.

²¹ Eh, poor us [have pity on us]. All together we made my sacred water [atole]. All gathered for your hand.

²² Very close to your feet [you enter], you see your food bu'ul-il-wah [literally, "bean tortillas"], your food-leaf covered with meat [meat tamales], your tamales with gourd seeds. Very close you enter, you see them.

²³ Look, see your food with Our Lord [Hachäkyum]. Look with the god pots for the god's assistants. Look, then, Older Brother of My Lord [Sukunkyum].

²⁴ Eh, it is good they make the sacred water [atole]. It is good I make it. All is gathered in your hand. . . .

²⁶ Eh, newly made tortillas [nahwah], they made white water [atole], newly they made it, then.

²⁷ Eh, there. My sons are all together. All together they pay for their welfare [their cures], my payments [offerings].

In this manner, accompanied by this prayer, each of the god pots is fed from the baskets of nahwah. As the feeding of the god pots is concluded, the ritual hosts once again step out of the god house and make a ritual offering of nahwah to the gods of the forest by throwing bits to the four cardinal directions.

When this final offering is completed, the nahwah and beans are divided among all those present in the god house clearing, men, women, and children. Thus, as do their gods, the Lacandon participants eat the symbolic substance of human flesh that has been dipped in symbolic human blood, the red bean sauce made from annatto. By early evening, the food had been consumed, the god house cleaned up, and the ritual participants returned home. The ritual was complete.

It is in the ritual offerings described here that the Lacandon have symbolically continued ancient patterns of human sacrifice and bloodletting. Systematic observation of Lacandon ceremonies and a familiarity with their mythic history makes it quite apparent that the red dye annatto represents blood in a variety of ritual situations, while food offerings of corn represent human flesh. And it is through the offering of k'ik' and xikals of incense that the Lacandon continue to practice, in symbolic form, the centuries old sacrificial rituals of the Nuki Nahwahto', their prehispanic ancestors.

CHAPTER NINE

Rites of Birth and Death

Thus far I have described the balché ceremony, the most common Lacandon ritual; one variation of the balché rite, the nahwah ceremony; and explained the social functions of these rituals together with the ancient patterns of sacrificial symbolism preserved in these ceremonies today. The same structural framework of these rites is found in a variety of other rituals. For example, ceremonies such as the *ya'ahk'in* or *na'ahplil,* which are opportunities for ritual payment to the gods after they have cured a serious illness or assisted during the birth of a child, are as structurally similar to the balché rite as is the nahwah ceremony. But there are two rituals that do not follow this pattern. These rites are the *mek'chul* and the Lacandon funeral ceremony.*

THE MEK'CHUL CEREMONY

The *mek'chul* is a ceremonial initiation into adulthood that involves a parent's ritual payment to the gods for allowing his child to survive. The name *mek'chul* comes from the Mayan word *mek'-ik* (to embrace), and refers to the way a mother carries her infant—that is, tied with a sash straddling her hip. The ceremony is both an initiation into adulthood and the occasion for a major ritual payment to the gods. Offerings usually consist of balché, incense, bark cloth headbands, k'ik', atole, and nahwah, as well as special ritual items that are chosen in accordance with the sex of the child sponsored in the ceremony.

The ritual offerings are presented by the father of the child to benevolent gods who have cared for the child from birth, as well as to appease angry gods who might want to harm the child in the future. Boremanse writes (1978:80):

Indeed, the father of the child will pay all the gods who helped or threatened his child at different periods of his life, i.e. every time he was seriously ill, at the meek'chahal [mek'chul]. This means that these gods

---

*I have not personally witnessed the mek'chul ceremony. My account here is based on information taken from the fieldnotes of Dr. Michael J. Rees, the Ph.D. dissertations of Dr. Didier Boremanse (1978) and Dr. Dale Davis (1978), and information provided by Lacandon informants.

have sometimes to wait for ten to fifteen years before they get the gifts which have been promised to them when the father was burning incense in their censer and working over his sick child with the xate leaf. But at last the promise is fulfilled.

Although the father does not necessarily act as the child's sponsor during the ritual, selection of a child's ritual sponsor is his responsibility. For example, Dr. Michael J. Rees was asked to sponsor a child's mek?chul ceremony in the community of Lacanha Chan Sayab.

The mek?chul is really a two-part ceremony. The first part involves a payment to the gods and lasts for several days. The second part involves the ritualized instruction of a child and lasts less than an hour. Although the mek?chul of the Yucatecan and southern Lacandon Maya is performed when the child is an infant, the Lacandon of Najá usually wait until the youth is a teenager. Two young men I questioned about the mek?chul rite said their ceremonies had been performed when they were approximately sixteen years old. But there are young men in Najá about that age now who have not yet been through the rite.

Why do the northern Lacandon wait so long to hold the ceremony? Boremanse speculates that the parents are afraid the child may not live, so they choose to wait until it is strong and healthy "because there would not be much sense in paying the gods if they did not keep the child alive" (1978:91). But this does not explain why parents wait until the child is an adolescent instead of conducting the child's mek?chul when he is five or six years old.

The principal reason for delaying the ritual expressed by my informants was simply, "I am lazy." This statement reflects the fact that preparation of a mek?chul ceremony is so much work and expense that sponsors often delay this task as long as possible.

Postponing a mek?chul ceremony also functions to keep a child in a state of relative dependency on his or her parents, for a person traditionally cannot marry or participate in balché rites until passing through their mek?chul ritual. When a child leaves home to start his own household, his natal household loses a working member—that is, there are fewer hands to work in the milpa and help with household chores. Therefore, if they choose to do so, parents are able to prolong the dependency of their children. A father can refuse to give his daughter away in marriage because she has not been sponsored in a mek?chul rite. It is also difficult for a son to marry and leave his parents if he has not had his mek?chul ceremony because he cannot begin the religious practices required of an adult married man. One example of this predicament can be viewed in a Lacandon family in which the head of the household is an elderly man in his eighties. Despite his age and physical frailty, this man must continue to work a milpa large enough to feed the ten dependents in his immediate family. Although his eldest unmarried son is about seventeen years old and hoping to marry soon, his father has not yet arranged for a mek?chul ceremony. In my opinion, his father is deliberately postponing the ritual in order to maintain his son's dependency because he needs his son's help in the milpa. By postponing the mek²chul and thus delaying his son's marriage, he can prolong his son's role as a supporting member of the household.*

Along with the ritual offerings of balché, incense, bark cloth headbands, rubber figures, nahwah, and atole, special objects used in the child's ritual instruction are placed before the god pots one day before the instruction phase of the mek²chul. If the mek²chul is for a boy, these objects consist of sets of bows and arrows, a leather pouch, a net bag, a machete, a gourd bowl, and a gourd plate containing flints, feathers, a knife, and cord. These are the traditional tools of the adult Lacandon man. Even though Lacandon men now hunt with rifles, bows and arrows are still used in the ritual. The objects on the gourd plate—flints, feathers, knife, and cord—are the materials used to make bows and arrows. The machete and net bag are for work in the milpa.

The night before the child's instruction, his or her father begins to make ritual offerings to the god pots, burning incense and k²ik², and feeding the god pots nahwah and balché. Boremanse (1978:95) recorded the following ritual prayer, which is recited at the time this set of offerings is given to the god pots. Items in brackets are my additions to the text.

> This Känänk'ax [Guardian of the Forest] is the rubber of my Kayum [the name of the boy to be instructed the following day], from me to you, and for the Lord Ki Chäk Chob [Äk²inchob, god of the milpa]. Go and see him and you will tell U Na'il Yum Bilil Ka'an [the wife of Hachäkyum, Lord of the Sky] to see my Lord from your part. You will then go to Itsanok'uh [Alligator Lord, guardian of lakes and maker of hail] and tell him, "This is for you my Lord, he will not have to bury him, he is happy." Forgive my Kayum for him to get up and collect *pom* resin because he will be in good spirits. Get rid of his stomach aches so that he can eat. Then he will be in good spirits to get up and burn incense. I will not have to bury him. Send your word, this is from me to you, go and see, o Lord, and you Ki Chäk Chob, go up and see u Yum Bili Ka'an, go and see him with Äk Nah [Our Mother, the moon], see, see what is being done, and cure my Kayum, I will not have to bury him.

The following day, about an hour after sunrise, the men begin to drink balché so that when the ceremonial instruction starts, everyone is slightly inebriated. At this time, women also gather in the ritual cooking huts near

---

*This speculation was based on observations made in the spring of 1982. Subsequent events, described to me in the summer of 1983, support this line of reasoning. During my absence, Chan K²in's son had received his mek²chul, married a young Tzeltal Maya woman, and was doing bride service in his father-in-law's village. But at the same time, Chan K²in had arranged the marriage of his oldest unmarried daughter to a young man from Mensäbäk. This young man had joined Chan K²in's household and was performing his own period of bride service. Thus, Chan K²in allowed his son to marry in circumstances that created no shortage of labor for his own household.

the god house and partake of the balché provided by their husbands. After the offerings of nahwah and xikals of incense are given to the god pots, the initiate is brought to the god house. He wears a new xikul called *hach nok'* (real clothes), which has been spotted with red dots using annatto dye, possibly to simulate either ritual bloodletting or the pelt of a jaguar. The young person is brought into the god house and led to a hammock hung especially for him in the northeast corner of the god house. He is told to watch the approach of the ritual instructor's wife, who is allowed to enter the god house at this time.*

The man who performs the ritual instruction then offers a bowl of balché to his wife as she enters the god house repeating the phrase "Now I am very drunk" several times. (Although ritual inebriation is necessary for spiritual purity and thus is a desirable state during ceremonial activities, balché has a low alcohol content so it is unusual for anyone to get very intoxicated.) The instructor then informs everyone present that he is going to take the child and the period of ritual instruction begins.

The first phase of the instructions deals with how to climb a tree in case of attack by a dangerous animal. Taking the young man by the hand, the instructor leads him to the northwest corner of the god house, squeezes the child's legs around the corner support and says, "Learn how to climb a tree, climb a tree. Do not learn from me, I do not climb trees, do not learn from me." Next, the instructor sweeps the floor of the god house and the shelves where god pots are stored when not in use while saying, "Learn to sweep the shelves of our Lords. Do not leave anything. Do not learn from me, I do not sweep the house of our Lords. You learn how to clean it even though I do not."

In the next phase of ritual coaching, the instructor picks up the set of bows and arrows, net bag, and machete that have been prepared as offerings and placed in front of the god pots. He steps out of the god house with his wife and the initiate following behind. The rest of the ritual participants remain in the god house. At the edge of the god house clearing, the instructor demonstrates how to use the bow and the type of arrow to be used when hunting different species of game. Next, the child is shown the path to his household's private latrine area (each household group has two private latrine areas, one for men and another for women), because it is considered bad manners to defecate in any other spot. The instructor then shows the initiate a path to his family's milpa and the trail leading to the grove of pines where the family's copal incense is tapped.

Once the instructions for tapping incense have been received, the initiate is taken to a nearby stream and told about carrying water for balché. He is instructed to be careful with the *pak* (the large clay pot with the face of Bol) because water to make balché is carried in this pot and

---

*This is one of the few occasions when a woman is allowed in the god house. When a boy is going through the mek'chul ceremony, a woman has no active part in the ritual, but if the rite is held for a girl, then a woman performs the ritual teaching.

balché is served from it during ceremonies. The group then returns to the god house clearing, where the young man is shown the balché chem, the dugout canoe used to brew balché. Next, they reenter the god house and the initiate is shown how to make arrows using the implements left on the gourd plate the previous day—the knife, feathers, and cord.

Finally, the initiate is given a gourd of balché to drink (his first official drink of balché), and the instruction period ends with a lecture admonishing the child to be thoughtful. The word for thought, or thinking, in Lacandon is *tukul,* and the following short speech is recited so that the child "ma' u tubul u tukul" (does not forget to be thoughtful). The instructor touches gourd seeds to the child's forehead, neck, and chest, and says:

> Here is calabash for your thoughts. Do not learn from me, I do not have any for my thoughts. For you there are calabash seeds for your thoughts, for you to remember, for you to remember everything. Whatever you do, for the things you do, you will think about them, because here are [seeds] for your thoughts. Do not learn from me, I am thoughtless. But there are [seeds] for you to think about your work, about whatever you do.*

The child is then given nahwah, the instructor saying, "Here, for your thoughts, some food for you; there is nothing more" (Boremanse 1978:99). This brings the ritual instruction to a conclusion. The father of the new initiate chants over him while touching him with a xate' leaf and saying:

> O Lord Ki Chäk Chob, I have finished sponsoring my Kayum, I will not have to bury him. He will burn incense on the stone in your house. O Lord Känänk'ax, send forth your hand to cure him. You have just seen his arrows, you have just seen the *chäk hu'un.* You saw what has been done, first for Itsanok'uh. I will not have to bury him, he will walk and bring the first of my *chäk hu'un,* give tortillas to your censer, to you shrine. O Itzana, tell Chob, tell Itsanok'uh . . . and tell T'uup. He will come down and tell Yum Bili Ka'an and u Na'il Yum Bili Ka'an: He will not have to bury his child Kayum who will pray to his censers, who will give us the *chäk hu'un* of the *Na'abil-il.* Now you will go in and sit down Itsanok'uh. His smoke will be finished; finished will be the many rubber figures, to bring the *mek'chul* to an end, the payment of tamales. . . . This is the payment of their curing, their payment.†

This concluding prayer highlights the principal purpose of the mek'-chul rite, which is to pay the gods for having taken care of the man's son Kayum. At this point, Kayum is ready to assume adult roles and responsibilities. In the prayer, the gods who have cared for Kayum are

*Boremanse 1978: 98–99.
†Ibid., p. 99.

named, and Kayum's father is careful to point out all of the offerings he has presented to these gods during the course of the rite, and promises that his son will continue to make offerings to these gods in the future.

Two characteristics of this ritual instruction are also of special interest. First, the initiate is an adolescent and so already knows the ritual informa- tion that is imparted to him at this time—that is, how to work in a milpa, what arrows to use in hunting, and where the trail to the latrine area is to be found. Second, the instructor demonstrates the ritualized information while simultaneously denying his own experience in these matters. For example, while demonstrating how to climb a tree, the instructor is simultaneously telling the initiate "Do not learn from me. I do not climb trees, do not learn from me," and so forth.

At the conclusion of this prayer, the young man or woman returns to the hammock which has been hung for them in the god house while the father distributes balché to everyone present. The chäk hu'un tied around each of the god pots as an offering is distributed among the men and each puts one of the red bark bands around his head, except for the new initiate, who receives three of these headbands. Nahwah is then distributed to everyone, and the ritual participants eat, drink balché, and continue to make offerings to the god pots in the typical balché ritual pattern. The following day, this session of ritual instruction is repeated in exactly the same manner as the events of the first day described above.

The mek'chul rite is also performed for young women. The form of the ritual is identical to that which is held for young men, except the in- structions to the child are given in the ceremonial kitchen hut next to the god house, and the items placed in front of the god pots are the household tools used by an adult woman. Items used in a young woman's ritual instruction are spindles of cotton, thread, parts of a loom stored in a large gourd, a net bag with a water gourd, a wooden comb, and a gourd bowl. There is also a broom and a small table on which tortillas are made. The woman who sponsors the young girl will show her how to sweep the floor and take her to paths around the village, instructing her on where to fetch water, the location of the women's latrine area, and other such pieces of information. In the ceremonial kitchen hut, she is shown how to weave and told to wash her hands and cooking implements before preparing food. At the conclusion of the instruction period, as with young men, she is given a gourdful of balché to drink and her father chants over her. Again, as with the young men, the young woman receives ritual instruction in tasks that she is already quite familiar with. By the time of her mek'chul, a woman has been weaving, making tortillas, and performing other house- hold tasks for several years.

The mek'chul ceremony is not an isolated rite practiced only by the Lacandon. On the contrary, it is commonly found in different forms in a variety of Mayan societies and was almost certainly practiced by the Pre- hispanic Maya. Landa (Tozzer 1978:105–106) wrote of a Maya ritual that he called a "baptism" that was held for adolescent children. Features of this rite sound similar to the contemporary Lacandon mek²chul, including the presentation of gifts and offering of "wine" (presumably, balché) to the gods.

As Landa was writing about the Yucatecan Maya of the sixteenth century, and the rite is found throughout the Mayan area, it is interesting to compare the mek²chul with the *hetzmek,* the contemporary Yucatecan Maya version of the rite. Although the hetzmek has incorporated a variety of Hispanic features, on the whole it remains fundamentally similar to the Lacandon mek²chul.

Unlike the Lacandon of Najá (but similar to the practice of the southern Lacandon in Lacanha Chan Sayab), the hetzmek is performed when the child is an infant, less than a year old. A sponsor is asked to perform as an instructor for the infant, but acceptance of this role is also considered acceptance of the role of godparent (compadre, comadre) to the child. The institution of *compadrazgo* is Hispanic and involves the sponsor in a greater level of responsibility to the child and his parents than is accepted by a Lacandon child's sponsor. The Yucatecan hetzmek is also a secular activity that takes place in the infant's home, whereas the Lacandon mek²-chul is a religious event—a time of payment to the gods—that takes place in the god house.

As in the Lacandon ritual, a man and wife act as sponsors for the child; but in the Lacandon rite, only one person plays a major part—a man if the child is a boy, a woman if the child is a girl. In the hetzmek, women play a more prominent role. Also, unlike the Lacandon mek²chul, the hetzmek is a private family matter and outsiders are not invited. The persons attending the rite are seated around a table on which are placed objects for the child's future life such as a book, pencil, notebook, catechism, hammer, hatchet, tortillas, a plate of boiled meat, and money. Other objects are placed under the table. The ceremony was described in this manner (Redfield 1962:189):

> The godfather takes the child and puts it astride his hip. He then goes nine times around the table, at each circuit taking one of the objects from the table and putting it into the hand of the child while he utters an admonishment according to the character of the object. Thus, on the first trip around the table he takes up the book, and says, "Here you have a book. Take it so that you may learn to read." Thus he does with each object—the pencil and the notebook, so that the child may learn to write; the catechism, so that he may learn to pray; the hammer, that he may learn to work; the hatchet, that he may learn to fell bush; the bread, that "he may learn to eat everything"; the boned fowl, that he may learn to eat "good food"; the coins, that he may learn to earn money. He then hands the child to the godmother, telling her to make hetzmek with it and she does as he has already done. It is also customary for the

godmother, on each of the trips around the table, to eat one of the nine squash seeds which have been placed on the table. "As the squash seed is opened to expose its soft interior, so will the mind of the child be opened." When the squash seeds are used up, the godmother has finished her task.

Although the concept of godparentage is culturally Hispanic, the form of the hetzmek and the pattern of ritual instruction closely correspond to the Lacandon rite. In both ceremonies, the child is instructed in the responsibilities of an adult and shown the tools that will be a part of his or her adult life. And just as the Lacandon sponsor gives the child squash seeds and admonishes the child to be thoughtful, during the hetzmek squash seeds are opened and eaten to ritually open the mind of the child. The principal differences between the two rites are the ages at which the child is sponsored and the fact that Lacandon women do not play a large role in the mek'chul ceremony for young men, whereas Yucatecan Maya women have a role in the rites for both boys and girls.

DEATH AND LACANDON FUNERALS

The funeral is the other Lacandon ritual not structured in the same pattern as the balché ceremony. Funeral rites are not held in the god house as might be expected. In fact, funerals are the only Lacandon rite in which the god pots are excluded from the ritual because they must be covered and protected from the malevolent spirits that roam about after an individual's death.

According to Lacandon mythology, men did not originally have to die. A mythic character named Nuxi (Ancient One) or Ah Lehi Kah Bäh (Trapper of Moles) is said to have traveled to the underworld and there met and fell in love with the daughter of Kisin (the god of death). In the underworld, he was given the *asab,* a device that allowed him to awaken the dead and give them new life. The part of this myth provided here describes Nuxi's use of the asab and how it was rendered useless, thus ensuring that all humans must die. Items in brackets are my additions to the text.

> The Mole Trapper saw one of his companions thinking of his wife who had died. Nuxi said, "I am very sorry for you. Let us go and see her. If you have your wife's clothing bring it."
>
> His companion answered, "I have her clothes, I shall bring them." Arriving where her bones were the Mole Trapper unwrapped his *asab,* "the Awakener," and inserted it into her nasal fosa. Soon after he had inserted the *asab* she arose sneezing. Her flesh, her skin, the hair of her head, she had them all.
>
> Her voice came forth, "Oh I am so tired of sleeping." But she had no clothing. The Mole Trapper said to her husband, "Come and give her

clothing." The man's wife took and put on her clothing, then returned home with her husband.

In this fashion the Mole Trapper resurrected two people. But when he went to tap his incense trees his wife unwrapped that which he kept covered [the asab]. She saw it. She called all of her companions to look at that which Nuxi used to raise the dead.

The *asab* he used to awaken us had colors, like the lotus flower. They were bright red. The one for men was a paler tone; the one for women was a brighter red.

When Nuxi returned from tapping his incense trees he saw something was wrong. "Oh you have unwrapped my things." His wife answered, "No, I didn't uncover them." "You unwrapped them. I see it. I am going to die because of this. But me, I shall not burn in the underworld. You shall burn." She answered again, "No, I did not uncover them."

Another day, one of Nuxi's companions came to his house. He asked Nuxi to raise his wife who had died some time before. The Mole Trapper answered, "Very well. Let's go. Bring her clothing."

Nuxi dug up her grave, pulled out her bones, and fit them all together loosely. He put on her skull. He said to her husband, "Turn your back, do not watch." He inserted the awakener into her nasal fosa . . . but this time nothing happened.

The Mole Trapper said, "Oh my wife unwrapped it. This is not good. Now I know I am going to die."

In a month he was no more. He burned with fever and died. But he was not concerned about dying. He wanted very much to return and see the daughter of Kisin.*

The Lacandon believe that death is caused by the gods, although it is not an end to life but a transformation to another level of existence. This follows the same principle of reversal that causes transformations in the ritual offerings. For example, a small amount of sour balché becomes a large amount of sweet balché and copal incense is transformed into tortillas when fed to the god pots. The ritual principle operating in this belief system is that reversals occur when an object changes levels of the universe. The Lacandon believe in a multilayered universe (see Figure 6.1), which corresponds to the Prehispanic Maya belief that both heaven and the underworld were multilayered (Coe 1980:151). In Lacandon cosmology, the first layer of the universe is the underworld, called *Metla'an*. The second layer is the surface of the earth covered with jungle and inhabited by humans; the third layer is the sky where Hachäkyum and the other celestial gods live; the fourth layer is the home of the deity K'akoch, who is the creator of the gods; and the fifth and remotest layer, which is

---

*This myth was recorded and translated by Robert Bruce. He provided me with a copy of the myth during one of his trips to Najá in the fall of 1982.

cold and dark, is the home of the Chembel Kʾuh. It is the change from one level to another that causes a reversal of form. Thus, death is a reversal of life, the transformation that a living organism undergoes when alternating between levels of existence.

If a man angers the gods, they may punish him by sending sickness to a member of his family. Through divination, a man attempts to learn which gods are angry, the reason he is being punished, and which gods will consent to help him. Once this information has been established, the divination continues to discover what types of payment the gods will want if they choose to help him.

Someone sick or in trouble will ask an older male relative to conduct a divination ceremony for him. The diviner goes off by himself into the jungle to ask questions of the gods using one of two methods that provide answers to yes or no questions. The first method involves placing the fingers of both hands together with the fingernails touching. The hands are then brought sharply together, palm to palm, and the answer to one's question is read from the position of the fingers. The second method of divination involves rolling two xate leaves in a special pattern. The answer to the question is read in the pattern in which the leaves unravel.

Hachäkyum is the ultimate arbiter in decisions of life and death. If mercy is granted, a person will be cured. If, despite offerings and prayers, the person dies, his soul *(pixan)* goes to the underworld to be judged by Sukunkyum, the chief Lord of the underworld and older brother of Hachäkyum. If a person is guilty of theft, lying, or murder during his or her life, then Sukunkyum gives the soul to Kisin (the god of death) for punishment. Kisin, in turn, alternately burns the mouth, eyes, ears, and anus of the soul with hot iron and freezes it with cold water. If a person's sins are very bad, the soul may be burned and frozen until nothing remains. The judging and punishment of souls is described in the Lacandon myth "U Kʾakʾil Metlaʾan" ("The Fires of Metlaʾan"). I have provided a translation of portions of this myth from Bruce's (1974: 258–274) original Mayan transcription of the tale. Because Lacandon myth tellers assume that their audience already knows the story, narrative details are often omitted. In this translation, I have added bits and pieces of background information that a Lacandon audience would take for granted to make the story easier to follow. The numbering of the lines of text follows Bruce's original transcription. Items in brackets are my direct additions to the text.

1 In the beginning, Sukunkyum [Lord of the underworld] said to a Lacandon man, "Go see the fires of Metlaʾan, and the irons that will burn you.

2 Arriving, the man was shown [the underworld]. Sukunkyum said, "See it? Do you see it?"

3 There were pieces of iron near the mouth of the fires of Metlaʾan. Sukunkyum showed them the iron. "Look! Do you see the iron [to burn]

for your ears?,", and he showed them one. "This is the iron [to burn] for your mouth. Here is one, the iron for your eyes. Here is a piece of iron to burn your urethra . . . because you saw [slept with] your older sister, your younger sibling, your mother . . . [this iron] is to burn you all. For those who see their younger siblings, their mothers, their older sisters . . . there is another piece of iron to burn their anuses, because your friends had affairs with them."

⁴ Sukunkyum spoke again, "I have shown you. [Now] Let's go to my house. Tomorrow the soul of one of your friends is going to arrive."

⁵ The man answered, "Good. Tomorrow you will show it to me."

⁶ [The next day] the soul arrived. He was brought [to Sukunkyum's house] by Kisin [the god of death].

[When Kisin and the soul arrive at Sukunkyum's house, he is not home. Sukunkyum has left to lower the sun into the underworld, where he will feed and carry it through the underworld so that it can rise again with renewed strength in the morning. When he returns home, Sukunkyum is tired and hungry and is beginning a meal when Kisin and the soul interrupt him.]

⁹ Kisin arrived and said, "Give it [the soul] to me."

¹⁰ Sukunkyum answered, "I am hungry. Wait, I am eating."

¹¹ Kisin said, "No! Give it to me!"

¹² Sukunkyum paused in finishing his meal. He gazed at the soul. He gazed into the eyes of the soul. He saw many things the soul had done. He saw that it had seen [had an affair with?] its younger sibling.

¹³ Sukunkyum gave the soul to Kisin, he said, "Take it. It is yours."

¹⁴ Kisin was very happy. He answered, "Eh good. I'll take it." He took the soul. He grabbed the soul's hand. The soul [resisting] sat down. Kisin said to the soul, "Let's go!"

¹⁵ The soul said, "I will not go."

¹⁶ "LET'S GO NOW!" said Kisin, and he jerked the soul up. The man watched Kisin pull the soul over the edge [into the underworld].

¹⁷ Sukunkyum said to the ancient one [the Lacandon observer], "Let us go and watch. I will return for my food. Let us go watch how the soul is burned."

¹⁸ The man answered, "Let's go."

¹⁹ Kisin, Sukunyum, the man, and the soul all left together and arrived at the fires of Metla'an.

20 Then the Mole Trapper [the ancient one, the observer] saw Kisin take the iron. He saw him burn the soul with iron. It was then that he saw how Kisin did it.

21 Kisin took the ear of the soul. Kisin said to the soul, "You did not listen to the words of your father or mother," and he burned the ears of the soul.

22 Then Kisin said to the soul, "Your eyes were angry. You watched your father with your mother, and your friends. Your eyes were angry," and he burned its eyes with the iron.

23 Then he put the red hot iron on the soul's mouth. Kisin called, "Feel it! Do you feel the pain? You lied to your father and your friends."

24 The soul said, "Enough—What Pain! I will not do it again!"

25 Kisin answered, "[It is too late] You did this long ago. You answered [talked back to] your mother."

26 Again he burned the soul's urethra with red-hot iron. He burned it with hot glowing iron.

27 The soul said, "Aay! That is enough!"

28 Kisin said, "How does it feel? You did things to your little sister. That is not acceptable!"

29 The soul answered, "I will not do it any more, I will not be irresponsible!"

30 Kisin answered, "You did this long ago with your younger sibling, when you were still alive."

31 The soul answered, "No! I will not be irresponsible."

32 Kisin answered, "No more! You are to be totally burned up," and grasped the soul by the hand and pulled him into the middle of the fires of Metla'an.

33 The soul cried, "Uyi! My burning is very painful!"

34 Kisin answered, "If your burning is painful there is the freezing cold water of Metla'an nearby," and he threw it into the cold, cold water in Metla'an.

35 The soul said, "It is very cold, good!"

36 Kisin said, "The cold is good?" He threw the soul into the fire of Metla'an.

37 [The soul cried], "My burning is painful!"

38 For the second time Kisin answered, "Your burning is painful? There! . . . . the freezing cold water of Metla'an.

³⁹ Then Kisin pulled the soul out and threw it into the fire. He pulled it out a second time, and threw it into the freezing cold water . . . until it became small like a cricket. . . . Then Kisin pulled a second soul in. The first soul was totally consumed in the fire. [Changing it] Kisin pulled the soul of a chicken out of the fire.

⁴⁰ Sukunkyum said, "You see how your souls will emerge from the fire. Kisin pulls out horses, he makes dogs of your souls. Cattle will emerge . . . Now no people are created from your souls."

⁴¹ "If you kill your friends, you will not emerge, you will all go, finished in the fires of Metla'an."

⁴² Now Sukunkyum said to the Mole Trapper, "This is what you tell to your friends. Now go, go to my house."

Contrary to the account above, if a person's soul is judged acceptable by Sukunkyum, it will travel in a journey to the house of Mensäbäk, the god of rain, where it will live until Hachäkyum next decides to destroy the world. At that time, everything but the gods will be destroyed.

Although living with Mensäbäk is not a punishment, souls are thought to be unhappy because there is no forest or game. One may see animals, but there are only beans and tortillas to eat, because what you see are the souls of animals that cannot be killed a second time. Souls of the recently deceased often miss their home and family and desire to return to the land of the living. Mensäbäk then sends the homesick soul to look at its decomposing corpse, asking the soul if it really wants to inhabit this body. This sight is said to scare a soul so badly that it then accepts its fate.

Kisin can also cause death. The Lacandon believe that just as everyone has a *pixan*, or spirit double, so too the soul has a counterpart in the form of a spider moneky that lives in the underworld. In search of meat, Kisin hunts these monkeys, and if he kills one then the person who has that monkey as his pixan's double will also die.* Thankfully, Kisin is not successful every time he hunts and often misses his target. But if he wounds a pixan's spider monkey double, the person on earth will feel a corresponding pain in the same part of the body where the monkey was injured. For example, while working in his milpa one day, a Lacandon man was hit on the head by a falling tree branch and knocked unconscious. Later, he explained this incident by saying that Kisin must have been hunting and hit the monkey that was his pixan's double. Laughing, he said he was lucky that Kisin had not hit the monkey hard enough to kill it, or he, too, would have been killed.

Although death is an ending for a person on earth, according to Lacandon mythology, it is just the beginning of a journey one's soul must

---

*This belief in an animal spirit companion is found throughout Latin America in a variety of forms. For example, descriptions of these beliefs for the Zinacantecan Maya and the Yanoma- mö can be found in Vogt (1970: 11) and Chagnon (1983: 104).

make through the underworld. On this journey, a soul faces several trials. First, it must pass down the road to the underworld encountering chickens, lice, a pack of dogs, and a large river that is not really a river—it is the tears that the soul's family and friends have cried in their grief. To reach the underworld, the pixan must successfully pass these obstacles, so a person is buried with food for this journey, candles for light, and wood shavings with which to build a fire. To further aid the soul in its encounters, a corpse is buried with an ear of maize to give to the chickens in the underworld, a handful of hair for the lice, and bones to throw to the wild dogs so that it will not be eaten. Finally, the soul of the dead person's favorite dog helps him cross this obstacle by letting its master's pixan hold onto its ears as it swims across the river.

The Lacandon also have a myth that describes this journey through the underworld. Called the "Ancient One Who Saw the Underworld," the myth provides an account of the Lacandon's concept of the underworld and describes what happens after a person dies. I have provided my translation of Bruce's (1974) transcription of this myth. As in the previous myth, items in brackets are my additions to the text.

1 In the beginning, Sukunkyum [Lord of the underworld] said to the ancient one, "Let's go, I will show you something to tell your friends about."

2 The ancient one answered, "Good, let's go."

3 He saw the beautiful forest in the Underworld. He saw boar in the Underworld and having arrows he shot at them.

4 He did not know it was the spirit of a boar. He shot it but he could not kill the spirit.

5 He saw deer, mule deer, pheasant, turkey, partridge, all of the animal spirits. He saw the spirits of spider monkeys. He saw howler monkeys, night monkeys, snakes and jaguars.

6 The ancient one said, "Eh, there are many hidden animals in the forest here!" Then he said, "I did not know that these were spirits of animals."

7 Sukunkyum said to the ancient one, "They are animal spirits. They are all the spirits of animals. Do not shoot the animal's spirits for they will not die."

8 They arrived at a path. [Sukunkyum said] "This is the path you take when you die."

9 The ancient one was shown [the places he would have to pass]. "Here are dogs. First you will see many dogs."

10 Next he saw chickens. He walked ten steps and arrived at [the place of] chickens. He passed the chickens, passed them.

¹¹ The place of lice was far away.

¹² He took ten steps and came to water. He saw a river.

¹³ Sukunkyum said, "Eh, here comes your soul. Do you see it? Watch how it passes."

¹⁴ The soul passed them on the road.

¹⁵ "First the dogs . . . Do you see how the soul throws animal bones to the dogs? If you have no bones the dogs will eat you" [said Sukunkyum].

¹⁶ The ancient one saw the dogs come and the soul threw the animal bones. As the dogs finished eating the animal bones the ancient one watched the soul run past. The dogs finished. The dogs saw the bones and finished them as the soul ran past.

¹⁷ The soul arrived at the place of chickens. He took corn [he carried], threw it to the chickens, then passed by.

¹⁸ He arrived at the place of lice. He threw the hair from his head and passed by.

¹⁹ When the soul arrived at the water his dog came. The dog arrived and said to the soul, "What do you see here Master?"

²⁰ The soul answered, "Nothing. I cannot cross the water. It is very deep. The current is strong and there are extraordinary alligators."

²¹ The dog answered, "You poor thing. Lie on my back and grab my ears. I will pass you over the water," and they passed by.

²² Sukunkyum said to the ancient one, "Someone goes to my house." [In other words, another soul has just arrived in the underworld.]

²³ Another soul came down the path. First it arrived at the water. Then its dog came.

²⁴ The dog said to the soul, "What do you see Master?"

²⁵ The soul answered, "Nothing. I cannot cross the water. It is very deep, the current is fast, and there are extraordinary alligators."

²⁶ The dog answered, "I am not sorry for you Master. You cut my ears, you cut my tail, and you did not like to see me. I have no ears. I have no tail [and thus the master has nothing to hang on to]. I will not help you pass. You must cross the river alone."

²⁷ The soul said, "I cannot cross! I will not cross. There are extraordinarily many alligators."

²⁸ The dog answered, "Watch me cross. Did you see it? Nothing will eat you. There are no alligators."

²⁹ Sukunkyum said to the ancient one, "None of the dogs will bite you. The chickens will do nothing to you.

³⁰ None of the lice will bite you. They only frighten your soul so that it will not try to return.

³¹ There is no water. There is no river. Your spouse is crying, all of your friends cry.

³² [Because your friends cry] You see a great river and your soul sees alligators in the river. There are no alligators. It is to scare your soul so that it will not return [to the living]."

³³ Now Sukunkyum said, "Eh go. Go with the soul of your friend to my house.

³⁴ You see now how you will pass on the road of death."

³⁵ The ancient one answered, "It is true Lord!"

After overcoming the underworld's obstacles, the soul is judged and sent either to be punished by Kisin or to live with Mensäbäk. At this time, the last obstacle the soul must master is to conquer their fear of Mensäbäk's pets—giant jaguars, snakes, and eagles that the pixan must feed for the god of rain. In fact, the souls have nothing to fear because they are actually in no danger. Mensäbäk's pets will not eat them, because being spirits they have no scent.

A DEATH IN THE VILLAGE

The following is an excerpt from my field diary.

> January 1985. It is cold and damp tonight. I couldn't sleep, and could hear Chan K'in Viejo was still up, so I went to sit with him by his fire. I have never seen him so despondent. The death of his eldest wife (Koh) seems to have drained him of spirit. He is just sitting, staring into the fire.
>
> I have been in and out of Najá for five years, but this night, sitting with Chan K'in by his fire, has been the most moving experience I have ever had here. It is hard to describe my feelings tonight. I have spent a couple of hours listening to Chan K'in pour his grief out. He is particularly concerned that he will not see his wife again in the afterlife when he dies and we talked about what she must be experiencing now on her journey to Metla'an. So I sat with him tonight while he cried. I have never seen a Lacandon man express such emotion so openly. We talked about his wife, about death, and what may lie beyond death. He told me about the journey a soul has to make through Metla'an after death, and we talked about the soul's life with Mensäbäk after they have completed the trials in the Underworld.

Philosophical questions about life and death must be universal. His grief really struck a chord in me with Mom's death being only a year or so ago. Maybe that's why he felt free to talk with me—he thought I might understand. Whatever the reason, I feel deeply honored he chooses to talk with me tonight. I can't get over it—middle of the jungle, middle of the night, I sit around a fire with this ancient Maya man and talk of life and death.

A whole other issue bothering Chan K²in is that K²in Pannia Agua says he has seen Koh's spirit by his house. K. P. A. woke me up last night, visibly shaken, to tell me Koh's spirit had been scratching on the walls of his house. This is serious because the spirits of the dead are malevolent. Lonely and missing their families they come back to take a loved one with them into death. It must feel horrible to be grieving over a death, but then believe their spirit is wandering around at night threatening to take you with them. The spirits of the dead are supposed to like hanging around their families. If Koh's spirit doesn't leave everyone in peace Chan K²in Viejo may have to move his household to a new location. Though I have known about this belief for awhile I have never given it much thought. It is eerie now to be faced with a number of people who are really scared about something I have not taken seriously.

When a person is dying, village life continues as usual until the time of death is near. As death becomes imminent, all men in the village go to the god house to pray and burn incense. As the person lays dying, the eldest man in the family will sit by his or her side praying constantly, touching the dying individual with a xate² leaf that has been passed through the smoke of an incense offering; this is the same behavior observed when attempting to cure someone who is seriously ill. At the time of death, an ear of maize is placed in the corpse's left hand for the chickens in the underworld. A lock of hair is cut from the deceased's head and, together with a bone, is put in the other hand as an offering to the lice and wild dogs believed to be in the underworld. The body is then put into a hammock with the knees bent and arms crossed across the chest, and the hammock is tied shut with a cord. When a woman dies, all of her jewelry and other personal adornments are removed at this time. Finally, the eyes of the corpse are closed so that the pixan does not come back and call the living to follow it.

After preparing the body, men go to the god house and put all god pots on the storage shelf, placing an ear of maize beside each incense burner. The god pots are then covered with palm leaves and the god house is swept clean. This action is taken to protect the god pots from the malevolent spirits that will be around the village for the next five days. The Lacandon call these spirits *Kisin,* which refers not only to the god of death, but to malevolent spiritual beings in general. After a death in the village, the spirits most feared are the *Kisin Aak²ä,* or "Night Kisin," who are believed to dwell underground, look like rats, and try devouring corpses in the grave or small children wandering alone in the jungle. The ear of maize placed with the god pots is to protect them, because when a Kisin sees an ear of corn, it perceives the maize as a crowd of people; being afraid of crowds, the Kisin will leave the god pot alone. (Ears of maize are also hung on the balché chem and in the rafters of the god house.) The god pots must be protected because if a Kisin touched a god pot, the pot would lose its spiritual power. Thus, they remain covered for the five dangerous days after a funeral.

The night of a death, a clay brazier with charcoal is placed under the corpse in the hammock to keep it warm. If this is not done, the soul of the deceased might complain that his body was cold, and as punishment, the gods might cause another member of the family to die.

The following day, friends of the family go to the cemetery and dig a grave. Only a few feet deep, the grave has a thatch or corrugated tin roof about four feet high erected over it. When the roof is finished, the hole is covered with poles and the grave is ready to receive the corpse.

In preparation for the burial, two men carry the body to the cemetery. The corpse is carried in its hammock slung from a pole passed through the ends of the hammock, which the pall bearers rest on their shoulders. The funeral procession is led to the cemetery by the men carrying the corpse and followed by others bringing food and personal possessions of the deceased that will be buried with the body. As they walk, men converse with the corpse, describing what is happening. When I asked why people talk to the corpse, I was told the body must be spoken to at each stage of the funeral ritual so the spirit does not later return to frighten its surviving family.

Arriving at the graveyard, the poles covering the grave are moved aside just enough to allow the body to be lowered into the hole. The ends of the hammock pole rest on the edges of the grave, so that the body lies suspended in its hammock not touching the ground. Before the poles are replaced to cover the grave, a net bag containing *ma'ats* (a drink made of water and corn dough), tortillas, candles, and shavings of firewood, is put into the dead person's lap. The food is for the pixan to eat on its journey through the underworld. The candles and wood are to provide the soul with light and warmth on its journey. The body is suspended in the grave with its head to the west and feet to the east, but with the head raised so that the corpse faces the east. Boremanse (1978) says the corpse is buried facing the east so that it faces Yaxchilan, the home of the gods. It is also likely that corpses are laid to rest facing the east as a symbol of rebirth. They face the rising sun, which, in Mayan belief, dies at sunset, travels through the underworld as a skeleton at night, is resurrected, and rises in the east the following day. Thus, burial facing the east symbolizes the Mayan belief in the soul's life after death.

Once the body is placed in the grave, the poles are laid over the hole and covered with palm leaves. The palm leaves are then covered with a mound of earth about a foot high. At this time, each member of the family says goodbye to the corpse saying, "Now I am going to throw earth on your face. I prayed to the gods but you did not recover. I do not know which gods were angry" (Boremanse 1978:120). Once the grave has been filled in, ashes from the fire used to keep the body warm the previous night are spread over the grave mound to prevent maggots from infesting the burial. It would be disrespectful if there were maggots inside the grave; the deceased's soul might be angered, which again could bring misfortune to the living.

A variety of grave goods including both food and the deceased's personal possessions are left at the gravesite. Food is left both inside and outside of the grave for the two stages of the soul's journey. The food placed in the lap of the corpse is for the first stage of the soul's journey through the underworld. A plate with tortillas and ma²ats is also hung on the west side of the grave above the head of the corpse from the rafters of the shelter built over the grave. This food is left outside of the grave for the soul to eat during the second stage of its journey as it travels from the underworld to the house of Mensäbäk, where it will live after death. After burial, the pixan is believed to return to the burial site and partake of the food left at the grave for four days, and fresh food is left for the soul daily. On the fifth day, the soul no longer returns and the period of ritual danger ends.

Several items, including the deceased's personal possessions are also left on the grave mound. Palm leaf figures representing dogs are left on the burial mound at the corpse's head and feet. These are said to accompany the soul through the underworld to the river of tears. At the river, the soul of the dead person's favorite dog will meet him or her to carry its master across the river. The family and friends of the deceased also stick candles into the ground around the periphery of the grave so that the soul will continue on its journey to the underworld. It is believed that if these candles are not provided, then the soul will linger around the gravesite. K²in Pannia Agua, the man scared by the ghost of Chan K²in Viejo's wife Koh (described in my field diary) had not burned these candles at her grave and thus was susceptible to supernatural harm from her spirit. As the candles are placed in the ground and lit, the person bringing the candles prays aloud, asking the soul to leave them alone. For example, when I performed this rite I was instructed to say:

He²ah kib	Here is your candle
Ma² ha²as-ik in wol	Do not frighten me
Cha-ah ah kib	Take your candle
Tak wa tu kin man, ma	If I am passing,
ma ha²as-ik in wol	do not frighten me

In Lacandon symbolism, candles invariably represent death, especially in dream symbolism. To dream of a star or a macaw (because of its red breast) prophesies death because both are symbolic of funeral candles.

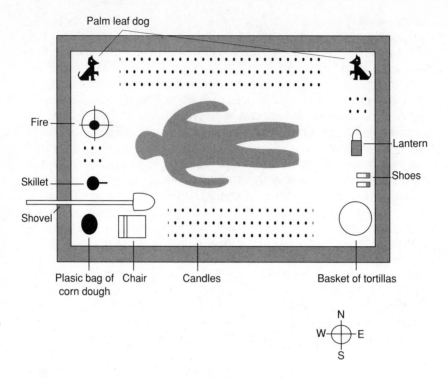

Palm leaf dog

Fire

Skillet

Shovel

Plasic bag of corn dough

Chair

Candles

Basket of tortillas

Lantern

Shoes

N
W—⊕—E
S

F I G U R E 9.1 *Diagram of a Lacandon grave mound*

As I participated in the funerary rites for a woman, the goods left at the gravesite reflected her roles in life. Along with the candles and palm leaf dogs were placed a skillet, her favorite chair, her shoes, a kerosene lantern, and a plastic bag of corn dough (Figure 9.1). Other gravesites in the cemetery had different objects. The graves of several children had toys left on the grave mounds, and those of adult men often had machetes and other tools, as well as their shoes and remains of food offerings.

Finally, a fire is built next to the grave so the soul may rest and warm itself on its return journey from the underworld. After the funeral, when the mourners return from the cemetery, everyone bathes and changes clothes. This is done because the earth of a grave is believed to have a smell that attracts the dead; they might come to call another person to join them.

It is thought to take the soul three days to travel to the underworld and then back on its way to the house of Mensäbäk. These three days are a dangerous time for the living, because the soul may reappear in places it used to frequent, and to see the soul of a dead person can itself cause death. During these three days, the food on the grave must be renewed every day. It is expected that the food will have been touched on the first day, for the soul has not yet reached the underworld and so may have eaten. On the second day, if the food is not touched, it is believed that the soul has not yet returned from Metla'an. If, on the third day, no food has been taken at all, it is surmised that the soul was not allowed to leave Metla'an and has been completely burned by Kisin.

Just as the god pots must remain covered on their shelf for five days after a funeral, so too there are certain prohibitions that must be followed for the same period of time. If a man has died, men cannot make arrows during this time. If a woman dies, other women may grind corn only at noon. Women also may not comb their hair or weave, and the floor of the house may not be swept during this period. If one of these restrictions is violated, it is believed that another person will soon die.

The range of Lacandon rituals has now been examined. The balché is a key ritual, forming the pattern around which most other Lacandon rituals are structured. It is also a ritual of intensification, a social gathering where gods and men get drunk together, social tensions can be dispelled, and traditional lore and knowledge may be shared and reinforced.

The mek'chul rite is "a ritual of integration" (Boremanse, 1978: 124). In this ceremony, an individual is initiated as an adult member of Lacandon society, and becomes socially and ritually mature. In addition, it is the occasion for a major payment to the gods when the sponsor of the ritual makes generous offerings on behalf of his child.

Finally, the funeral is a "ritual of exclusion" (Boremanse, 1978: 124). It is the only ritual in which the god pots do not play an important part in the ceremony. The gods are covered and survivors prohibited from working at their everyday tasks for several days. During the funeral, members of the village gather around the grave to say goodbye and leave gifts, but they ask to be left alone because their departed loved one is now a dangerous spiritual force that could also kill them. Thus, the funeral is the occasion in which the living separate themselves from the dead, asking the soul to stay away and not return to harm them.

CHAPTER TEN

🌿 Lacandon Culture and the Future

Over the last twenty years, the belief that the last traces of traditional Lacandon religious beliefs and practices will disappear with the death of the village elders has developed among people who have worked with the Lacandon. In particular, this sentiment is focused on Chan K'in Viejo, who is the religious specialist in the community of Najá. Perera (1988) offers a particularly good example of the social importance writers have assigned to Chan K'in Viejo. Often, the degradation of the Lacandon's forest environment by Mexican lumber and petroleum industries is used as an analogy for the process of cultural disintegration that is presumed to be occurring among the Lacandon today. This view has been strongly expressed by Gertrude Duby-Blom, and in the work of Perera (1988) and Boremanse (1981). For example, this analogy is stated in Harris and Sartor (1984:32) when Dr. James Nations, quoting J. E. S. Thompson writes: "The old ways of the Maya, as J. Eric Thompson put it, 'melted like snow in the hot rays of technological materialism.' Simultaneously, the Lacandones began to lose the rainforest environment that had supported both the old ways and their lives." This comparison is made even more explicitly by Perera (1988:41) in the following passage:

> My previous four visits to Nahá have been laden with signs of a progressive cultural disintegration. Apart from the proliferation of radios, trucks, tinned foods, cosmetics, and novelty-store geegaws are the subtler, unspoken defections from an ancient way of life. Each member of the community—not excepting Chan K'in [Viejo]—seems to suffer from some form of psychic arrest caused by the felling of the trees and all the evils attendant on the despoliation of the forest.

The common belief that Lacandon culture is disintegrating and soon to be lost forever is a reflection of the opinions held by the three elders of Najá. Because these three men are respected authority figures and ritual specialists of the village, their opinion is persuasive. I unquestioningly accepted this perspective myself for the first year I lived in Najá. Chan K'in Viejo, for example, would make comments such as, "My sons are lazy. They do not know the old ways and do not learn the old songs." Similarly, in a videotaped interview, anthropologist Mike Rees recorded the following conversation with another community elder, Mateo Viejo.

Rees: "In twenty years there will be other men in the god house and you will be dead. Do you think that when you are dead your son Mateo will throw them [god pots] out?"

Mateo Viejo: "I do not know. . . . It is very bad. . . . They [young men] are ashamed of the gods. My son Chan K'in is ashamed. He will throw them out."

There is no question that the community elders believe that when they are dead so, too, will the old ways (and, by implication, the *good* ways) die, and it is perfectly understandable that anthropologists with long-standing relationships with these men have echoed their perspective. But is this belief true? In the first place, it is my guess that elders feel their experience is neglected in virtually every society in the world. Furthermore, in preliterate societies such as that of the Lacandon, the total inventory of cultural information must be memorized and repeated in every generation. Given the nature of the mechanisms that exist for preserving and disseminating information in this type of society—that is, through memory and word of mouth alone—traditional information is irretrievably lost in every generation. Consequently, what anthropologists have characterized as the degradation of Lacandon culture is actually a natural cultural process, intrinsic to preliterate societies, that has operated since human beings first acquired culture. This process is not bad in and of itself, it simply exists and is unfortunate only in that anthropologists cannot possibly record all available information as it changes, disappears, or is invented. Undoubtedly, traditional and esoteric information is being lost in the transition from older to younger generations of the Lacandon. But is Lacandon culture disintegrating? The answer to this question is not as clear-cut as some believe, and here, in the concluding chapter of this book, the future of Lacandon society is worth considering.

The phrase "degradation of Lacandon culture" usually refers to intergenerational changes in knowledge or utilization patterns of a variety of phenomena, including mythology, ritual behavior, esoteric incantations for healing and divination, and the use of plants and animals in the forest. In particular, when anthropologists working with the Lacandon bemoan the degradation of Lacandon culture, they focus on material or behavioral changes. For example, the Lacandon no longer weave their own cloth for their traditional garments (xikuls), but instead buy manufactured cloth. Or, the Lacandon no longer use thatch for roofing material, instead buying sheet tin to roof their houses. But does this signal the disintegration of their culture?

MEASURING FAITH

Having studied Lacandon religion and ritual, I was primarily interested in the question of whether the people of Najá would abandon their traditional beliefs and convert to Christianity when their village elders died. But I found the question of faith a difficult problem to investigate. Because the elders of the village are regarded as the faithful guardians of traditional beliefs, I sought to compare their knowledge of religion and ritual participation with that of younger men, assuming, as the older men had assured me, that the younger generation knew little of the traditional beliefs and cared less. Yet, when I questioned each young man in Najá old enough to participate in ritual activities about his knowledge of traditional rites, and after observing them all on numerous ritual occasions in the god house, it became obvious that generation was not an accurate criterion for judging the degree of an individual's faith in traditional religious beliefs. Based on observations conducted during communal rituals and what young men said in private interviews, it soon became clear that the younger generation's patterns of ritual participation and religious belief were indistinguishable from their elders, although, as I expected, elders had a more detailed command of ritual lore.

I next thought to use the utilization of modern medical facilities as a scale for measuring a man's faith in the non-Christian gods, because in the Lacandons' traditional belief system, disease is a punishment sent by gods and curing consists of identifying and appeasing angry gods through the offering of incense and balché. The problem with this measure of faith is that *everyone* in Najá makes use of the local medical facilities in addition to making offerings in the god pots when a family member is sick. Nations (in Harris and Sartor 1984:32), for example, describes an example of this behavior involving Chan K'in Viejo (I mention this example because, in most romanticized literature on the Lacandon, Chan K'in Viejo is the individual usually cited as a guardian of traditional Lacandon values, a heroic figure, trying to defend his people against the onrushing flood of technological change): "I once watched Chan K'in stand up from an ongoing curing chant, walk outside of the god house to accept an injection from a visiting Mexican physician, then return to his prayers to Hachäkyum, his chant stronger than ever and his god pots still blazing with copal." Viewing scenes such as this, it becomes clear that if Chan K'in Viejo takes advantage of modern medical technology, the use of medicine can be used neither as an accurate measure of faith in traditional Lacandon religion and therapeutic beliefs nor as an accurate indicator of loss of those beliefs.

It is also common for pregnant Lacandon women to now travel to the hospital in San Cristobal to deliver their babies. Only Chan K'in Viejo's wives still deliver their babies at home with the help of their co-wives. Thus, judging by acceptance of modern medicine and ritual participation, the younger generation certainly is not abandoning the old traditions. On the contrary, young men are adding modern features to traditional behaviors *by copying the behavior of their fathers* (such as supplementing traditional forms of healing with modern injections).

In this fashion, I narrowed the issue of faith to three principal questions:

1. Why do young men not take an active role in everyday ritual work?
2. Do the young men really not know traditional lore as the older men claim?
3. Do the young men really believe in the traditional gods?
   I set out to find the answers.

It is true that most young men do not tap incense trees for copal resin to supply incense for their father's god pots; neither do they make balché, although they readily participate in the rituals. When these men were asked the first question, "Why don't you gather incense and make balché?," the reply was invariably, "Ne ma? kol-en" ("I am very lazy"). The young men who were questioned certainly knew how to tap the trees for resin to make incense, and they knew how to make balché, but they almost never engaged in either activity. Of the twenty or so balché rituals in which I participated, Chan K?in Viejo, Mateo Viejo, or Antonio were the ritual hosts of fifteen. In most of the other rites, the ritual host was Kayum, the son of Chan K?in Viejo and son-in-law of Antonio.

Why do young men not do this work? The answer to this question is surprisingly easy. The young men do not do this ritual work because they are not required to do so. The reason they are not required to conduct these ritual activities is a consequence of the shift in settlement pattern that the Lacandon experienced in the early 1950s.

Traditionally, the Lacandon lived in isolated family clusters scattered widely through the jungle. When a young man married and completed his period of bride service, he took his wife and children and started his own independent family compound. As sole head of an independent household, it was this man's individual responsibility to care for his family's religious needs. In this role, he had to gather resin for incense, construct his own god pots, build his own god house, and make his family's balché. But this situation changed in the 1950s when Lacandon families began to live together in small communities to defend against the encroachment of outsiders. Over the past generation, the families in each community have intermarried, with the result that it is no longer necessary for each individual head of household to conduct all essential ritual labor by himself. For example, because there are two communal god houses in Najá, each individual man does not have to build and maintain his own individual god house.

In the case of Najá, virtually everyone shares an affinal relationship to the three community elders, Chan K?in Viejo, Mateo Viejo, and Antonio. Because of the large interrelated nature of their families, these three men not only are the undisputed leaders of the community but also they are the patriarchs of practically every family in Najá. Thus, when these three men conduct the religious affairs of their families, they automatically involve everyone else in the village as well. Examine, for example, Figure 10.1, which diagrams the interrelationships between two Lacandon patri-

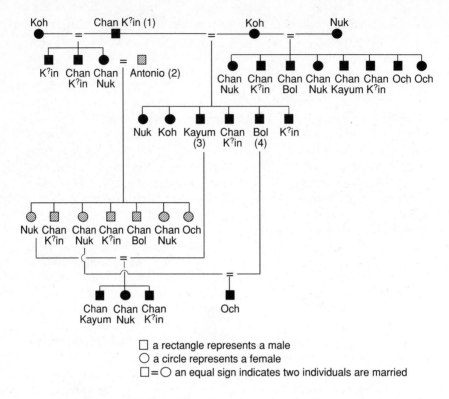

□ a rectangle represents a male
○ a circle represents a female
□=○ an equal sign indicates two individuals are married

FIGURE 10.1 *Interrelationship of two Lacandon families*

lineages. As illustrated in this diagram, the four heads of households (encompassing thirty-three individuals) are all related to Chan K'in (1). Men 3 and 4 are both 1's sons, and Antonio's (2's) sons-in-law, while Antonio (2) is 1's son-in-law. Traditionally, because all of these men are adults and heads of their own households, each would have built and maintained his own god house. But today, in the community setting of Najá, all defer to the authority of the oldest male relative. Thus, Chan K'in (1) has become the leader of ritual affairs for all of these men, and they worship in his god house. When Chan K'in dies, it is probable that Kayum (3) and Bol (4) will defer to the religious authority of Antonio (2), who is a village elder as well as their father-in-law.

In essence, the older men's complaint that the young men are lazy and no longer care about ritual duties is not a result of a negative change in Lacandon culture. This lament stems from the maintenance of a traditional pattern of behavior (eldest male in a family as ritual leader) in a community structure in which the old pattern is no longer necessary. The younger generation of men does not take responsibility for gathering incense, making balché, or hosting rituals because it does not have to; indeed, these younger men are not supposed to. Under traditional cultural rules, heads of households are responsible for religious duties. Because the three community elders are the heads of almost every extended family in Najá, the ritual well-being of their families is their responsibility, not the task of younger men. This conclusion is supported by private interviews with the sons of the village elders. For example, the older sons of Chan K'in Viejo and Mateo Viejo, all men in their late twenties or early thirties (and thus perfectly capable of conducting their families' ritual affairs) all said that when their fathers died, they were willing and able to take over the community's religious responsibilities, but that at the present time it was not necessary because their fathers did this work.

The second question—Do the young men really not know traditional lore?—is based on the older men's statements that the younger generation of men does not know the traditional myths and ritual songs. In fact, one reason that Chan K'in Viejo has been so receptive to anthropologists in the last twenty years is that many of us have been recording information that he believes will be lost when he dies. Although younger men certainly do not possess the incredible and encompassing knowledge of ritual and mythology that Chan K'in Viejo has memorized, they are not as remiss in their ritual responsibilities as older men believe.

Two examples illustrate this point. During a balché ritual, Chan K'in Joven, son of Chan K'in Viejo, was asked if he knew any of the traditional songs. In an offhand manner, Chan K'in Joven replied negatively, but when pressed for a more complete answer he admitted he did know them but was embarrassed to sing them. At this point, two other men cut into the conversation to agree with Chan K'in Joven. They all knew the songs, they said, but just didn't like to sing them. Notice here that these comments were elicited during a ritual when the young men were in the presence of their community's elders. The operational principle here is not that younger men are ignorant, but that they defer to the knowledge of their elders when in the presence of these older men. Thus, a denial of knowledge is an act of self-effacement and respect when in the presence of a community leader, not necessarily an admission of ignorance.

Furthermore, Chan K'in Viejo's sons, despite what their father says about them, know the traditional mythology and songs quite well. Much of the material for Bruce's book *Lacandon Texts and Drawings From Nahá* (1976), a compilation of traditional Lacandon songs and poetry, was written for Bruce, in Mayan, by Chan K'in Viejo's sons Chan K'in Joven and Kayum, the only two men in Najá who know how to read and write. Bruce (1976:13) writes that Chan K'in Joven felt it was important to record this material: "[H]e told me he wanted to write down the texts of all his father's songs which he either had not yet learned in their totality, or those of which he feared he might forget some significant detail."

In the above passage, one can see an example of an attitude that directly contradicts the perceptions of the elders of the village. Chan K'in Viejo says his sons do not know the traditional lore. His son Chan K'in Joven agrees with him, yet at the same time is working to record and preserve the stories his father has taught him. Thus, contrary to the popular belief that younger men do not care about the old ways, one can see examples of how the younger generation is using newly adopted techniques (in this case, writing) to record and preserve the traditional information their fathers claim these same young men do not care about.

It is also important to remember that Chan K²in Viejo is a very old man, about ninety years old, and thus has had seventy years to develop his knowledge of Lacandon lore. It is unreasonable to expect younger men to equal his command of this material. Further, anthropologists have long realized that information in preliterate societies is plastic—that is, each generation adapts the lore of its forefathers to its own cultural circumstances, adding and subtracting bits and pieces of knowledge as time passes (see, for example, Ong 1982). It is only with the written word that information can be frozen in one form, and even then the meaning of words continues to change. Because almost no Lacandon mythology was recorded until Bruce's voluminous 1974 work, *El Libro de Chan K'in,* anthropologists really do not know how this lore has changed in hundreds of years of retelling. In fact, we really do not know how Chan K²in Viejo himself has inadvertently changed Lacandon lore in the past seventy years, although I do know that myths I recorded from Chan K²in Viejo in the early 1980s are slightly different than the same stories Bruce recorded from the same man a decade earlier.

The point here is that traditional lore changes with every generation. The process is inevitable in nonliterate societies. Chan K²in Viejo does not remember everything his father taught him, just as the current generation of young men does not remember everything their fathers have tried to teach them. Instead of bemoaning the loss of some idealized version of Lacandon mythology, it might be more useful for anthropologists to study the patterns in which this lore changes as it is transmitted from generation to generation, as well as how the newfound literacy of a few members of Lacandon society may even more profoundly change their culture.

The answer to the final question—Do the young men really believe in the traditional gods?—is more difficult to judge. By keeping records of activity in the god house, I know that every married man in the village occasionally prays there making offerings to god pots, and that all men attend the balché ceremonies. When asked directly if he believed in the traditional gods or if the old gods were real, each individual provided a positive response. Several of these men did express an uncertainty about how powerful the gods actually were, or if they listened to men's prayers, but they believed these beings did exist. When asked about Christianity, these men also refused to go along with my attempt to make them characterize one belief system as "true" or better than another. Most of them accepted that Jesus Christ is a god, but a foreign god, not to be worshipped by the Lacandon. I was told that Hachäkyum understands all languages (I had asked if one could pray to Hachäkyum in Spanish), and that it was our (foreigners') own fault if we no longer communicated with him. Thus, again, in contradiction to the statements of the village elders, younger men claim to believe in the old gods. Evidence such as participation in the balché rite and prayer in the god house support the statements of these younger men.

RETAINING TRADITIONS

In the light of the technological and cultural changes currently bombarding the Lacandon, as well as the invasion and degradation of their environment, it is reasonable to ask why the people of Najá have not followed the pattern set by their neighbors in Lacanha and Mensäbäk by converting to Christianity, cutting their hair short, and wearing pants and shirts instead of their xikuls. Why does the younger generation of Lacandon in Najá retain these traditional beliefs and practices? Brought from a virtual stone-age existence into the industrial twentieth century in the space of their own lifetimes, older men keep their traditions alive through a combination of faith and habit. For example, during an interview, Chan K'in Viejo once said that he sang the old songs and told the traditional stories because he hoped the younger men would learn them. He said he thought the god of foreigners [Jesus Christ] was a powerful god, but that what he had been told about Christ (that he would take all souls with him into the sky and could save them all from being burned in the underworld) was not true. "Äkyantho' and Jesus Christ are the gods of foreigners," he said. "Hachäkyum is the god of the Lacandon."

The attitude expressed above by Chan K'in Viejo is understandable in a village elder. But the younger men are products of the twentieth century; unlike their fathers, they have been brought up in an environment that is full of the influences of Christianity and modern technology. Why do they keep the old rituals and beliefs alive? The answer to this question is complex and revolves around three issues. The first of these issues is faith, and this has already been discussed. They continue to practice their traditional religion because they believe in their gods. The other two issues are quite different. But young Lacandon men also retain their traditional rituals and appearance because these factors make them special and exotic, and generate the demand for the items they sell to tourists, a lucrative sideline discussed in Chapter Four. Finally, maintaining these traditions helps support their distinctive ethnic identity. One can instantly identify a traditional Lacandon man by his dress and appearance. If a man cut his hair and dressed in pants and shirt he would lose this identity, becoming just one more of thousands of poverty-stricken Indians. On the other hand, as illustrated by the following anecdote told by Bruce (personal communication), Lacandon individuals are aware of and consciously manipulate their exotic image.

Bruce's story takes place in the southern Lacandon community of Lacanha Chan Sayab. Lacanha is composed of people from two separate villages who joined together in the early 1940s. The community was soon divided by a conflict between the two ritual leaders of the former communities. The conflict intensified, then abruptly ended when both men died, one soon after the other, leaving a leadership vacuum that no one filled. An American Baptist missionary stepped into this vacuum in the early 1950s (after failing to gain any converts in Najá) and convinced the people in Lacanha to abandon their traditional gods and rituals, exchange their traditional garments for pants and shirts, and ultimately convinced several men to cut their hair short. This, then, is the situation Bruce encountered, and his anecdote concerns an incident he witnessed while visiting Lacanha.

One afternoon, upon hearing a plane carrying tourists approaching to land at the community, the men who had not cut their hair rushed back to their homes, changed into xikuls, then ran back to the airstrip with sets of bows and arrows to sell to the visitors. In other words, even after their conversion to Protestant Christianity, some of the men of Lacanha continued to preserve the pretext of being traditional Lacandon in order to market their crafts to tourists. They were well aware that cutting their hair and dressing in pants and shirt would hinder the sale of crafts to gullible tourists, thus they preserved their exotic appearance.

Appearance is also an important component of a young Lacandon man's self-image. In response to my questions about cutting their hair and wearing shirts and pants, the general response I received from these men was that they did not want to look like *kah,* a derogatory term (derived from the word for town, *kahal*) that refers to people of Indian heritage who have abandoned their native traditions, in particular, the surrounding Tzeltal Maya. One young man told a story of attending a political rally to which the Lacandon had been invited; there one man from Lacanha (with short hair and wearing pants and shirt) was knocked down by a soldier and denied entry to the meeting because he was not recognized as a Lacandon. In fact, in an interesting reversal of my questions, several men suggested that because I was living in Najá, I should grow my hair longer and wear a xikul.

Several young unmarried men do wear pants and shirts when they travel to towns such as Palenque or San Cristobal for extended periods of time, although usually not in Najá (see Figure 10.2). When I asked about this practice, I was told that they changed in town because they felt this was more attractive to young women, and they did not like people attempting to look up their xikuls to see what they wore underneath. Despite this practice of clothes changing, in my ten years of experience I never saw a man from Najá permanently keep his hair cut short.

The final reason that young men continue to maintain traditional beliefs and practice traditional rituals is that these communal activities serve as a reassertion of the solidarity and distinctive identity of the Lacandon com-

FIGURE 10.2 *Three young Lacandon men in Palenque. Only K'in (far right) lives in Najá. He changed his clothes for the trip, but wears a xikul when in Najá.*

munity. This whole concept is encapsulated in a statement I recorded one afternoon near the end of a balché ceremony: "Hach Winik ("Real People"—that is, the Lacandon) know how to make balché, kah do not!" It is their religious beliefs and ritual practices that set the Lacandon apart, making them unique among the Maya Indians of Mexico, and they know it. Talking with men from the community of Mensäbäk reinforces their belief in the superiority of the old ways. From my own interviews with men from Mensäbäk, I found that many of them expressed dissatisfaction with their new religion (Seventh Day Adventism), which has restricted their consumption of traditional fish and game and banned alcohol, balché, and traditional music and dancing. Although they attended services regularly, some men apparently converted because their wives had joined the new church, or because they wanted to marry a woman who had already converted. A few occasionally visit Najá to drink balché, and many of them drink beer when they visit Palenque, violating the prohibitions of their new religion.

CONCLUSION

I do not personally believe the general prophecies of doom sounded by anthropologists who believe the Lacandon to be under the threat of cultural destruction. A representative example of this perspective is found in an article by Boremanse (1981:256), who writes:

> Chan K'in seemed quite happy with his life and not the least bit worried about the future. His father, Old Chan K'in, no doubt felt the change more painfully. The old man was doing his best to keep the traditions alive and preventing his people from yielding too quickly to the tempting and easy ways of acculturation, but he knew that he was fighting a lost battle. The world he was clutching at was drifting away and would soon be annihilated. . . . It seems now that due to the circumstances described above, the work of destruction which the Spaniards started some 450 years ago is going to be completed quite soon.

As I have illustrated, at least in terms of religious belief and practices, the Lacandon continue to be quite conservative in the face of a rapidly changing environment. Many of the changes in Lacandon culture have been superficial, such as the adaptation of new technology. When substantial changes have been made, as in the alteration of their traditional isolated settlement pattern in favor of small villages, traditional patterns of interaction and behavior have been preserved and adopted to the new environment while underlying behavioral patterns and social symbols have remained unchanged. A classic example of this phenomenon is the division of the principal god house in Najá. Traditionally, a man built his own god house and made his own personal god pots. In Najá today, the two most distinguished village elders, Chan K'in Viejo and Mateo Viejo share a god house, with Chan K'in Viejo "owning" the northern half, and Mateo Viejo the southern. Each keeps his god pots and conducts his personal rites in his half of the god house, allowing the respective sons and affines to utilize the space and ritual utensils in the appropriate family area within the god house. In this fashion, the traditional pattern of personal family ritual space and utensils has been not only preserved but also adapted to a larger community setting.

Lacandon Maya ritual behavior and symbolism have remained remarkably stable in the face of many changes. Old Chan K'in, the man Boremanse cites as "doing his best to keep traditions alive and prevent his people from yielding too quickly to the tempting and easy ways of acculturation," is indeed a ritual leader and vast storehouse of Lacandon religious lore. But as a young man, he was vigorously involved in the construction and sale of bows and arrows to tourists just as his sons today continue the same activity. I once witnessed this paragon of traditional virtues pay several thousand pesos for a portable AM–FM radio and cassette-tape player so he could listen to music with his wives. Obviously, as the examples above indicate, what many writers view as an ominous encroachment of technology into Lacandon culture, characterized by phrases such as "the tempting and easy ways of acculturation" or "novelty-store geegaws," do not necessarily lead to cultural disintegration. Elderly Lacandon as well as the young have quite readily adopted new technology as it has been made available to them.

Some cultures are stronger and more resistant to change than others. The Lacandon Maya have retained their traditional dress, appearance, rituals, and mythology after almost 500 years of acculturation by Hispanic society. Lacandon culture, as evidenced by the persistence of its traditional rituals and symbolism, is stronger than realized by the prophets of their demise. As exemplified by rites such as the balché and the mek²chul, the Lacandon continue to practice the rituals and worship the gods of their prehispanic ancestors.

The conclusive link between the Lacandon and these prehispanic traditions is their bloodletting and human sacrificial symbol complex. Once a basic part of ancient Mayan ritual, these practices are still symbolically repeated in contemporary Lacandon religious rites. The human body is represented by nahwah, k²ik² and xikals, with human blood represented by the ritual use of red vegetable dye; all together, they form an important set of offerings to the traditional Lacandon deities that, in the case of food items, are divided and consumed by the assembled ritual participants. Thus, the Lacandon are, in a sense, a window to the past.

One tenet of anthropology is that cultures cannot remain static. The Lacandon, no matter how much some may dislike it, are quickly being enveloped by the twentieth century. Their traditional isolation can no longer be maintained with the opening and exploitation of their forest environment. Yet despite the changes, if one looks closely at the Lacandon, it is still possible to see Mayan life as it may have been before the Conquest, even as they adapt rapidly and, I believe, remarkably well to pressures that have destroyed many other aboriginal cultures.

Mayan Texts of Lacandon Myths and Prayers

Note about transcriptions: In several places, I have extensively quoted myths transcribed by Bruce (1974). In Bruce's original transcriptions, he wrote the suffix [ah] (used as a past tense marker by placing it at the end of verb stems), as [a]. This causes some confusion when using verbs that end with "a," or when writing the word *a,* which also means *you* or *your.* To mark verbs in the past tense, I have written this suffix [ah] instead of Bruce's original [a]. Thus, for example, the verb *to make (ment-ik)* is written *mentah* in the past tense rather than *menta,* and *your* is written *a.* For example, *your father* is written *a tet.*

CHAPTER 2, pp. 20–21: U Tsimin ti² Hach Winik (Horses for the Lacandon)

¹ Hachäkyum tu meentah tsimin ti² hach winik. Tsimin tu yan meentah Hachäkyum.

² Tu meentah wakäx. Tu meentah kay k²ek²en. Tu meentah pek². Tu meentah miis, to meentah ulum yetel kax. Tu meentah yetel Äkyantho².

³ Äkyantho² tu meentah ti² kah tsimin. Tu meentah wakäx . . . Äkyantho² yetel Hachäkyum.

⁴ Tu meentah äh meh, tu meentah chibuh, tu meentah pek², tu meentah miis, tu meentah ulum, tu meentah kax, tu meentah kay k²ek²en ti² kah.

⁵ Tu meentah ta²k²in ti² wes.

⁶ Tu meentah ts²ak. Tu meentah yah-il yetel ts²ak. Hachäkyum ma² u mentik. Äkyantho² tu meentah tu wolol yahil.

⁷ Ts²ok u meentik Äkyantho² yetel Hachäkyum, tu ts²a²ah ti² hach winik.

⁸ Tu ya²alah Hachäkyum "He² tsimin; mak-eh, känänt-eh, uk²uls-eh, hans-eh.

⁹ He² k²ek²en. Tech kay k²ek²en. Tech ah kax . . . ulum. Läh ch²a²-eh."

¹⁰ Tu ch²a²ah; tu makah. Hach winik tu läh puuts²ah. Sa²asih, läh binih. Läh bini tu k²axil bäk²il. Pek² läh bini k²ax.

¹¹ Äkyantho² u k²ubiktik ti² kah. "He tsimin, wäkäx, kay k²ek²eken, meh, tu wolol tech. Läh känänte tech."

¹² Kah ne tsoy. Tu känäntah. Tu makah kay k²ek²en. Tu hich²ah tsimin yetel wakäx.

¹³ Tu wolol yäläk, tu läh känäntah. Tu läh hansah, tu yuk²ulsah.

¹⁴ Äkyantho? ne tsoy yol. Ma? tu puuts?ah.

¹⁵ Hachäkyum u ya?alik "?Eeh ne tsoy tech. Tsimin lati? yäh kuchi kah . . . bin et k?in.

¹⁶ "Wakäx, yan ti? u hit-ik che?. Yan ti? u bäk? ti? u chi?ik."

¹⁷ Äkyantho? u ya?alik ti? kah "Wakäx, yan a chi?ik u bäk?el. Tsimin, ma? a chi?ik u bäkel . . . ti? u kuch."

¹⁸ Tu ts?a?ah ta?k?in. "Ti a bo?oltik a winik ti? u meya ti? tech."

¹⁹ Äkyantho? u ya?alik "Yan humbuk?äb k?in, a pitik a wäläk?. Wakäx a he?ik. Tsimin a he?ik. Kay k?ek?en a pitik . . . tu wolol ah wäläk?. Ma? u puuts?ul. Sukhih. K?uchi humbuk?äb k?in, ne tsoy."

²⁰ Hachäkyum u ya?alik "?Eeh, bähe? ten, ma? tsoy.

²¹ Bähe?, mäna?an maska? ti?. Mäna?an maak ku bin u ku meentik maska? ti? . . . mäx baat.

²² Yan u käxtik tunich ti? u mentik u kol.

²³ Yan u käxtik u muul äh say. U päk?ik u nal yok?ol u muul äh say.

²⁴ Yan häläl . . . mäx ts?on. Bin u ku mentik chulul yetel tok?. Yan u bin u käxtik tok?."

²⁵ Äkyantho? u nukik "Ma?, Yumeh. Yan u bin u mänik maaska? . . . tumen ten, in läh eesik tu wolol ba?al meentik."

²⁶ Hachäkyum u nukik "?Eeh bay, tech. Ma? puuts?ih wakäx. Ma? puuts?ih u yäläk?. Tu wolol ba?al yan (ti? kah).

²⁷ Humbuk?äb ya? ax k?in yan u bin tu manän.

²⁸ Yan u meentik häläl, u kanik. Yan u meentik kib, kibil kab, u kanik. U ch?a?ik u baat . . . u ch?a?ik yetel kibil kab . . . yet u maska?. Tu wolol ba?al u mänik. Tumen hach winik, mäna?an ta?k?in . . . bin et k?in."

²⁹ Hachäkyum u ya?alik "?Eeh bay. Ne tsoy. Uts yan. Yan ch?och? . . . ?Eeh bay. Yan u hantik u taanin kun . . . u taanin che?.

CHAPTER 6, p. 60–62: Creation of the Earth

¹ Päytan K?akoch. K?akoch ma? lah u k?ul. Ma? yohel hach winik.

² Äk yum u yohel K?akoch. Lati?, K?akoch u k?ul.

³ K?akoch tu mentah lu?um. Ma? tsoy lu?um tu mentah. Ma? chich lu?um.

⁴ Mäna?an k?ax. Mäna?an tunich. Chen lu?um yetel ha? tu mentah.

⁵ Bähe? tu mentah k?in. Tu mentah äk na? ti? k?in.

CHAPTER 6, pp. 62–64: K?akoch tu mentah wolol K?uh (K?akoch made all the Gods)

¹ Bähe? tu mentah bäk nikte?. U sukun äk yum päytan toop?ih.

² Pach-il Äkyantho², Hachäkyum toop²ih.

³ Chen bäk nikte² tu yilah. Mäna²an k²ax. Ku yensik u yokol lu²um Hachäkyum, ya²alah "Ma² hach tsoy."

⁴ Sukunkyum ma² yemen ti² kula²an tu² to²op bäk nikte². Äkyantho² ma² yemen. Hachäkyum, lati² ne poch u yemen yok²ol lu²um.

⁵ Emi Hachäkyum, lik²i ch²iktal. Bin u ximbal ti². U t²änik u sukun. "Ko²oten käk ximbal teh äh kuyik wa ne tsoy lu²um." U sukun äk yum u nukik, "Bay, witsin."

⁶ Läh emi Sukunkyum yetel Äkyantho². Bäk nikte² tu p²ätah, toh yahaw. Man. Yilik. Way käbal xokol ha².

⁷ Päytan Hachäkyum tu yilah ti²an yatoch yetel Sukunkyum. Hachäkyum u ya²alik "Lati² ah katoch, tin t²an."

⁸ Sukunkyum u nuk-ik, "Ma² in wohel."

⁹ Hachäkyum u ya²alik, "Lati² äh katoch. Mäx winik."

¹⁰ Pachil u yilik K²akoch Hachäkyum. U t²an K²akoch ti² Hachäkyum. "²Eeh tech a watoch." Hachäkyum u nukik "²Eeh bay Yumeh."

¹¹ Ts²ok u tsikbal, bini K²akoch. K²akoch ma² u yeesik u bäh tu ka²ten.

¹² Yan oxtulo² yok²ol lu²um way. Yan tsikbal yetel oxtulo². Tu ya²alah "²Eeh, ma² chiich lu²um. Bik mentik²"

¹³ Hachäkyum u ya²alik "Bay, ch²ukteh in yan tukulik." Ne taki tan chumuk he²elel, u ya²alik Hachäkyum "Bin in kin käxtik ba²alinkil in mentik. Ko²ox." "Bay," u nukik u Sukunkyum.

¹⁴ Ti²an chichin puuk wits, tu ya²alah Hachäkyum "²Eeh sa²am. Päytan im pulik sa²am." Tu ch²a²ah sa²am, tu pulah he² yok²ol lu²um. "²Eeh, san sa²am chähih."

¹⁵ Bähe² Hachäkyum tu mentah k²ax. Ne tsoy . . . tu yilah ne tsoy. Tan u yilik hok²i tunich. Yan tunich yok²ol k²ax.

¹⁶ Tsok u mentik k²ax, tu wolol ch²ik binih. Bähe² ne tsoy lu²um.

CHAPTER 7, pp. 76–77: Text of a Lacandon incense-offering prayer

¹ He la² tech Itsanok²uh, he la² ah pom. Ch²a²e.

² U bo²oli ah t²an-ik wa yumbili ka²an.

³ Talak ma² siis u tukul ti ten.

⁴ Ma² cha²i-ik u hok²ol kan tu wa²an in bel tu k-in sutal.

⁵ Wa tech, wa talak teche yumen Itsanok²uh

⁶ Ma² cha²i-ik u hok²ol kan tu wa²an in bel kil in k²uchul tin watoch ti Najá.

⁷ He² la² tech u bo²oli la pome k²as ch²a²e.

⁸ Wa tech yet in yum.

⁹ He² la² tech u bo²oli pome.

¹⁰ Pul ah k²äb ah ki² kune.

¹¹ Talak yah in pach, talak wa ba² ta wil-ah ma² tsoy saasi ten.

¹² Tah wil-ah tah läk-il.

¹³ Ch²enen in pach, ka kunen.

¹⁴ Talak wa ba² ta wil-ah tin ment-ah saasi ten, ma² su²en . . .

¹⁵ Bähe² ma² su²en . . . ten ma² tin päyt-ik ah läk-il.

¹⁶ Ten ma² tin p²ast-ik ah läk-il, ten kin ts²ai-ik pom tech la hela². . . .

¹⁷ Ten netsoy in wil-ik ah läk-il.

¹⁸ Way k²uch en in wil-ik yalam ah watoch.

¹⁹ Tsoy kin bo²oli pom tech yumeh. . . . he² la² bo²oli pom.

CHAPTER 7, pp. 77–78: Text of a Lacandon balché-offering prayer

¹ He² tech yumen, he² tech ch²ulha² ki.

² Ileh yet in yum u na²il Äk²inchob.

³ Saasi-ten talak wa tah wuy-ah ba²alba

⁴ Mäna² in pach²-ik ah läk-il.

⁵ Ten tan in t²än-ik ah läk-il.

⁶ Talak wa ba² tah wil-ah ma²tsoy, saasi-ten.

⁷ Way yan-en, in ts²ai-ik tech balché.

⁸ He² tech Äk²inchob, he tech ch²ulha²ki.

⁹ He² tech Säkäpuk, he tech ch²ulha²ki.

¹⁰ Kune in yum Chan K²in.

¹¹ Lati² u yumbili-ech ah läk-il. Kunen u satal yol.

¹² Lukse! u sutuknak u yol, tian chäk yol.

¹³ Tah wil-ah to²on mäna²äk bubu²uk-tik balché. . . .

¹⁴ U tet in yum Chan K²in, mäna²äk bubu²uk-tik balché.

¹⁵ Tech ka²-tunt-ah uch-ik.

¹⁶ Talak wa ba² tah wil-ah, saasi ti in yum Chan K²in, saasi-ten.

¹⁷ Wa u ch²enen ti in yum Chan K²in la hela² yetel ch²ulha²ki.

¹⁸ Ah ka²-il-ik uhel balché, he² tech yumen.

¹⁹ He² tech ch²ulha²ki. . . .

CHAPTER 8, pp. 96–97: Nahwah offering prayer (Bruce 1974:320–326)

¹ He²la² Yumbil Mensäbäkeh!

² Ts²ibatnah he². Il-eh tun.

³ Ne ti² ku man u ximbal Säkapukeh!

⁴ Il-eh a wo²och wah. Il-eh tu² ho²ts²ulu².

⁵ Il-e yetel sil. Il-e tuun, u bo²oli kun yah.

⁶ Ka ch²a²ik lahe² la², ka bin ti² Nak²uh. Ka wokol ti².

⁷ He² bina²an hunts²itil, ²Itsanok²uh. Hunts²it ka ch²a²ik.

⁸ Ka ch²a²ik hunts²it, he² Na²-ten.

⁹ Ka bin ti² u Yumbili Ka²an. He² bina²an kex ti².

¹⁰ Kahin äh k-ile bin ho²ts²ulu. Sa²aseh! Ma² su² bin . . .

¹⁶ Il-eh Na²-el, il-eh! U Sukun in Yumeh! Na²-el-eh!

¹⁷ Il-eh Xk²anle²oxeh! Ki² Chäk Chob! Il-eh sikil wah ti² u Yumbili Ka²an.

¹⁸ Uts yan yäh men in ch²ul ha². Uts yan in wet hanan. Uts yan in paalal.

¹⁹ Läh mulik in paalal, läh mulik. Uts yän-in, Yumeh!

²⁰ Läh mulik-en-o². Mulik in wäh K²in. Mulik in wäh Chan K²in. Läh mulik-o² to²on.

²¹ ²Eh, ²otsil! Läh mulik yäh men in ch²ulha². Läh mulik ti² a k²äb.

²² Ne² ti² ka wok a wilik a wo²och bu²ulil wah, a wo²och muk-xiw-bäk², ah sikil wah. Ne ti² ka wok a wilik tuuneh!

²³ Il-eh! Il-eh a wo²och wah yetel Äk Yum. Il-e yetel sil-eh. Il-e tuun u Sukun in Yumeh!

²⁴ ²Eeh, uts yän-in yäh men in ch²ul ha². Uts yan ti² in meentah. Läh mulik tan [a k²äb]. . . .

²⁶ ²Eeh tumben tu meenta wah, tu meenta säk ha², tumben tu meenta tuun.

²⁷ ²Eeh le²! Läh mulik in paalal. Läh mulik u bo²olil kunyah, u bo²olil-en!

CHAPTER 9, pp. 108–111: U K²ak²il Metlan (The Fires of Metlan)

¹ Päytan Sukunyum tu ya²alah ti² hach winik "Ko²ox a wilik u k²ak²il Metlan, ti a wilik maskay ti² a welel-eex."

² K²uchi u yeesil ti² hach winik. U Sukun äk yum u ya²alik "Ileh a wileh."

³ Xok²ol yan, chi² u k²ak²il Metlan, maska². Maska² u yeesik Sukunkyum. "Ileh a wileh u maskay a xikin-eex." U yeesik hump²el. "U maskay a chi²-eex. He² hump²el, u maskay a wich. Hump²el u maskay u chuhik u cha-ch²ul-eex . . .

tumen ta wilah a kik, a wits'in, a na' . . . ti' u chuhik-eex, wa maak tu yilah u
yits'in, u na', u kik . . . uhel hunts'it maskay, ti' u chuhik u bäk'el a wit-eex, tumen
a bäh-eex a wet xileh."

4 Sukunkyum u ya'alik tu ka'ten "Tin weesah tech. Ko'ox in watoch. Saman ku
k'uchul u pixan a bäh-eex."

5 U nukik hach winik "'Eeh bay. Saman a tal a weesik ten."

6 U k'uchul pixan, u tal u päyik Kisin.

9 U k'uchul Kisin, u k'a'atik "Ts'a' ten."

10 U Sukunkyum u nuk'ik "Ne wi hen. Chukteh in hanan."

11 Kisin u ya'alik "Ma'! Ts'a' ten. Ma' tsoy Sukunkyum. Tan ti' hanan."

12 U Sukun äk yum u hämäch xulik u hanan. U cha'antik pixan. Ti' u wich u
cha'antik pixan. U yilik boom-ba'al tu meentah pixan. U yilik wa tu yilah u yits'in.

13 U k'ubik ti' Kisin. U ya'alik "Ch'a'eh. Tech yänin."

14 Ne tsoy u yol Kisin. U nukik "'Eeh Bay. Ten Yänin." Tu ch'a'ah. Tu ch'ukah u k'äb
pixan Kisin. Pixan kul uk bal. U ya'alik Kisin ti' pixan "Ko'ox!"

15 Pixan u ya'alik "ma' in tal."

16 "KO'OX KI'!" Tu hitah pixan Kisin. U yilik näk bini pixan, Kisin tu hitah.

17 Sukunkyum u ya'alik ti' nukuch winik "K'oox ah wileh. He' in wuul tu ka'-ten tin
hanan. Ko'ox ah wileh bik a welel-eex."

18 U nukik hach winik "ko'ox."

19 Yet bin Kisin yetel Sukunkyum, yetel hach winik, yetel pixan. K'uchi to'an u
k'ak'il Metlan.

20 Lati' äh Lehi Käh Bah kah tu yilah ch'a'e maska' Kisin. Tu yilah tu tokah maska'
pixan. Lati' tu yilah bik tu meentah Kisin.

21 Tu ch'a'ah Kisin tu xikin u pixan. Kisin tu ya'alah ti' pixan "Ma' tah wuyah u t'an a
tet, a na'." Tu tokah u xikin pixan.

22 Bähe' tu ya'alah Kisin ti' pixan "Ts'ik ah wich tu' ta päktik a tet, yet a na', yet a
bäh-eex. Ts'ik a wich." Pachil u wich u chuhik yetel maska'.

23 Bähe' u chi' tu käpah yetel chäko maska'. U t'änik Kisin "Uyeh ah wuye yah . . . ta
paytah a tet . . . ta paytah a bäh-eex."

24 Pixan u ya'alik "Ti'bil! Ma' samblen!"

25 Kisin u nukik "Uchul ka ta mentah. Ta nukah u t'an a na'."

26 Uhel u tokik u kuch'ul yetel chäko' maska'. U tokik chen chäk-t'inen maska'.

27Pixan u ya'alik "Aay! Ti'bil!"

28 U ya'alik Kisin "Ba'ik a wuyik? Tu meentah a wits'in. Ma' tu nupul yan!"

29 Pixan u nukik "Ma? samblen. Ma? su?-en!"

30 Kisin u nukik "Uch ta meentah yet a wits?in. Kuxa?an-eex toh."

31 U nukik pixan "Ma?! Ma?su?en!"

32 Kisin u nukik "Mäna?an! Tul a läh elel." U ch?ukik u k?äb. Tu wolol tu kap ch?intah tan chumuk u k?ak?il Metlan.

33 Pixan u ya?alik "Uyi! Ne yah in welel!"

34 Kisin u nuk-ik "Wa yah a welel? U siis-siis ha?il Metlan xok?ol yan . . . che? u tsok näk." U pulik yok?ol u siis-siis ha?il u k?ak?il Metlan.

35 U ya?alik pixan "Ne siis ki?!"

36 Kisin u ya?alik "?Eeh bay. Ne siis?" Tu kap ch?intah yok?ol k?ak?il Metlan.

37 Pixan "Ne yah in welel!"

38 Tu ka?ten Kisin u nukik "Ne yah a welel? Te? la?! . . . tu siis-siis ha?il Metlan."

39 Toh halik Kisin, u pulik yok?ol k?ak?. U halik tu ka?ten, u pulik yok?ol siis- siis ha? . . . tul u bin chichin ba?ik maas. Tu nah kap ch?intah. U ka?-halik Kisin u ka? pixan. U yankäch pixan, läh el-ih. Hok?i tu halah Kisin kaxil pixan.

40 Sukunkyum u ya?alik "Ah wilik bik u hok?ol a pixan-eex. Kisin ku halik tsimin, ku halik pek? a pixan-eex. U hok?ol wakäx . . . Bähe? mäna?an winik u hok?ol a pixan-eex."

41 "Wa ta kinsah a bäh-eex, ma? a hok?ol-eex. Ti? ka läh bin-eex . . . ts?okol yok?ol k?ak?il Metlan."

42 Bähe? u Sukun äk yum tu ya?alah ti? Äh Lehi Käh Bah "Yan a tsikbaltik a bäh-eex. Ko?ox. Ko?ox tin watoch."

CHAPTER 9, pp. 112–114: Nukuch Winik tu Yilah Yalam Lu?um (The Ancient One who Saw the Underworld)

1 Päytan u Sukun äk yum tu ya?alah ti? nukuch winik "Ko?ox in weesikech ti? a tsikbaltik a bäh-eex."

2 Tu nukah nukuch winik "Bay, ko?ox."

3 Tu yilah ne tsoy k?ax Yalam Lu?um. Tu yilah k?ek?en Yalam Lu?um. Yan u halal nukuch winik, tu hulah.

4 Ma? u yohel wa u pixan k?ek?en. U hulik, ma? u kimin u pixan.

5 Tu yilah yuk, tu yilah keh, k?ambul, koox, wan, tu wolol bäk? u pixan. Tu yilah u pixan ma?ax, tu yilah ba?ats?, aak? ma?ax, kan balum.

6 Nukuch winik u ya?alik "?Eeh, ne yan bakän bäk? yok?ol k?ax way!" Tumen u ya?alik "Ma? in wohel wa u pixan bäk?."

7 Sukunkyum tu ya?alah ti? nukuch winik "U pixan bäk?. Tu wolol bäk? u pixan. Ma? a hulik u pixan bäk?. Ma? u kimin."

⁸ K'uchi, u yeesik beh. "Lati' beh kah in kimin-eex."

⁹ Tu yeesah. "He' la' pek'. Päytan, pek' a wilik. Ne yaab."

¹⁰ Pachil, äh kax tu yilah. Tu ximbal tah. Ka'buk'äb tu hitah u yok, k'uchi to'an kax. Tu maansah kax, manih.

¹¹ Lati' bay, u naachil yän-in uk'.

¹² Ka'buk'äb tu hitah u yok, ha' tu yilah yetel uk'um.

¹³ Sukunkyum, lati' tu ya'alah "'Eeh, tak'al a pixan-eex. Ileh a wileh. Chantah wilah bik a man-eex."

¹⁴ Yok'ol beh u ch'äktik.

¹⁵ "Päytan pek' . . . ileh a wileh bik u pulik ti' pek' u baakel bäk'. Wa mäna' an u baakel bäk', u chi'ik-eex pek'."

¹⁶ Nukuch winik tu yilah u tal pek', (pixan) tu pulah u baakel bäk'. Xulih u hantik u baakel bäk' pek'. Tu yilah nukuch winik mani pixan. . . .

¹⁷ K'uchi to'an kax, tu ch'a'ah näl, tu pulah. Manih.

¹⁸ K'uchi to'an uk', tu pulah u tso'otsel u ho'ol. Manih.

¹⁹ K'uchi to'an ha', tali pek'. K'uchi pek', tu ya'alah ti' pixan. "Ba'alinkil ka wilik way, yaatsil?"

²⁰ Pixan u nukik "Mäxba'al. Ma' in ch'äktik ha'. Ne bulul ha'. Ne chiich yok ha'. Ne p'enk'äch yan ayim."

²¹ Pek' u nukik "Otsilech, in yaatsil. Täklen tim pach. Ch'uk in xikin. In maansikech tim pach ha'." La'eh manih.

²² Tu ya'alah Sukumkyum ti' nikuch winik "La'e bini tuun tin watoch."

²³ Huntul ku tal pixan. Päytan, k'uchi pixan to'an ha'. Pachil, pek' talih.

²⁴ Pek' tu ya'alah ti' pixan "Ba'alinkil ka wilik way, yaatsil?"

²⁵ Pixan u nukik "Mäxba'al. Ma' in ch'äkik ha'. Ne bulul ha'. Ne chich yok ha'. Ne p'enk'äch yan ayim."

²⁶ Pek' u nukik "Ma' otsilech, yaatsil. Ta xatah in xikin. Ta xatah in neeh. Ma' a k'at a wiliken.

²⁷ Pixan u ya'alik "Ma' in man! Ma' in ch'äktik. Ne p'enkäch yaab ayim."

²⁸ Pek' u nukik "Ileh in man. A wilik. Mäna'an u chi'ikech. Mäna'an ayim."

²⁹ Sukunkyum tu ya'alah ti' nukuch winik "Pek', mäna'an u chi'ik-eex. Mäxba'al u meentik kax te'ex.

³⁰ Uk', mäna'an chi'ik-eex. Chen ti'an u ha'asik u yol a pixan-eex. Tumen ma' u sut a pixan-eex.

³¹ Ha', mäx ha'. Mäna'an ukum . . . chen tu 'ok'nähih a lak'; tu 'ok'nähih tu wolol a bäh-eex.

³² Lati² ah wilik ch²ik yum uk²um, tumen a pixan u yilik yan ayim yok²ol uk²um. Mäna²an ayim. Tumen ti² u ha²asik u yol a pixan-eex. tumen ma² u sut a pixan-eex."

³³ Bähe² tu ya²alah u Sukun äk yum "²Eeh, ko²ox. Ko²ox ti²an u pixan a bäh-eex tin watoch.

³⁴ Ta wilah bähe² bik a man-eex yok²ol u beh kimin-eex. Yan a tsikbaltik a bäh-eex.

³⁵ Nukuch winik u nukik "²Eeh, hah, Yumeh!"

Ethnographic Films on the Lacandon

Early in the course of my work with the Lacandon I decided that ethnographic filmmaking should be a part of my documentation of Lacandon culture. As the idea for this book took form, I decided to film aspects of Lacandon culture that would supplement specific chapters of the book. I worked first with anthropologist Michael Rees and filmmakers Brian Huberman and Ed Hugetz. Later film was shot on my own, and with University of Southern California graduate student Michael Kruse. Altogether, between 1979 and 1985, we shot an estimated fifty hours of synchronous-sound film in Najá, and have produced three films. All films were shot with color super 8mm film, which was transferred to videotape for editing.

Using their footage, Huberman, Hugetz, and Rees have produced an hour-long documentary called *To Put Away the Gods*. At this time I have completed two ethnographic films on the Lacandon. The first, *Swidden Agriculture Among the Lacandon Maya* is on the slash-and-burn horticultural practices of the Lacandon and is meant to be watched in conjunction with Chapter Four of this text. Using long shots and minimal editing, the film follows one Lacandon family through a swidden season, captures their pace of life, and demonstrates the process by which they provide food for themselves while maintaining an ecologically sound relationship with their tropical environment. The second film, *The Lacandon Maya Balché Ritual* is about the balché ritual and should be viewed with Chapter Seven. The video shows all aspects of the ritual, from making balché, the ceremonial offering of the beverage to the gods, and ritual drinking by the men of Najá. In addition, several scenes show Lacandon watching a copy of the video and commenting on it. Both films are in color, about 30 minutes long, and subtitled in English.

Both the swidden and balché films are distributed by the University of California Extension Media Center in Berkeley. They may be purchased in any video format or rented in either ½ inch VHS or ¾ inch U-Matic formats. They can be rented or purchased by contacting:

University of California Extension Media Center
2176 Shattuck Avenue, Berkeley, California 94704
(415) 642-0460

Bibliography

ADAMS, RICHARD E. W.

1977   *Prehistoric Mesoamerica*. Boston: Little, Brown.

ADAMS, ROBERT M. C.

1973   *The Evolution of Urban Society*. Chicago: Aldine.

BAER, PHILLIP, AND MARY

1952   Materials on Lacandon Culture of the Petha Region. Microfilm *Collection of Manuscripts on Middle American Cultural Anthropology*, no. 34, University of Chicago Library, Chicago, IL.

BAER, PHILLIP, AND WILLIAM R. MERRIFIELD

1971   *Two Studies on the Lacandones of Mexico*. Institute of Linguistics, Publication #33. Norman: University of Oklahoma Press.

BAHR, DONALD, M.

1962   *Landa's Mayas*. Unpublished manuscript, Harvard Chiapas Project.

BARLOW, ROBERT H.

1943   *The Lacandon of the 1790's*. Tlalocan, 1:158–159, Sacramento: The House of Tlaloc.

BOONE, ELIZABETH H. (ED.)

1984   *Ritual Human Sacrifice in Mesoamerica*. Washington, D.C.: Dumbarton Oaks.

BORAH, W., AND S. F. COOKE

1963   *The Aboriginal Population of Central Mexico on the Eve of the Spanish Conquest*. Ibero-Americana, v. 45. Berkeley: University of California Press.

BOREMANSE, DIDIER

1977–78   "Northern Lacandon Relationship Terminology." *Saertryk Folk Reprint* 19–20: 133–149. Kobenhaven.

1978   *The Social Organization of the Lacandon Indians of Mexico*. Unpublished Ph.D. dissertation. Oxford: Oxford University.

1979   "Magic and Poetry Among the Maya." *Journal of Latin American Lore* 5(1):45–53.

1981   "Final Link with the Maya Indians." *Geographical Magazine* 53(4):250–256.

1983   "A Comparative Study of the Family Lives of Northern and Southern Lacandon Mayas of Chiapas. (Mexico)." *Journal of Comparative Family Studies*. 14(2): 183–202.

BRICKER, VICTORIA R.

1983 *The Indian Christ, the Indian King: Historical Substrate of Maya Myth and Ritual.* Austin: University of Texas Press.

BRUCE, ROBERT D.

1967 "Jerarquia Maya entre los dioses Lacandones." *Anales del Instituto Nacional de Antrolopogia e Historia* 18:93–108.

1968 *Gramatica del Lacandon.* Mexico D. F.: Instituto Nacional de Antrolopogia e Historia, Dept. de Investigaciones Anthropologiacas, Cordoba 21.

1973 "Figuras Ceremoniales Lacandones de Hule." *Boletin INAH,* Epoca 2(5):25–34.

1974 *El libro de Chan K'in.* Mexico City: Instituto Nacional de Antropologia e Historia.

1976 *Lacandon Texts and Drawings from Naha.* Mexico City: Depto. de Linguista, Museo Nacional de Antropolgia e Historia.

1976–77 The Popol Vuh and the Book of Chan K'in. Mexico City: *Estudios de Cultura Maya,* vol. 10.

1979 *Lacandon Dream Symbolism.* Mexico City: Ediciones Euroamericanos.

BRUCE, ROBERT D., AND VICTOR PERERA

1982 *The Last Lords of Palenque.* Boston: Little, Brown.

BURNS, ALAN F.

1983 *An Epoch of Miracles: Oral Literature of the Yucatec Maya.* Austin: University of Texas Press.

CALETTI, AUGUSTIN VILLAGRA

1949 *Bonampak La Ciudad De Los Muros Pintados.* Mexico City: Instituto de Antropologia e Historia, S.E.P.

CARASCO, DAVID

1984 *Quetzalcoatl and the Irony of Empire: Myths and Prophecies in the Aztec Tradition.* Chicago: University of Chicago Press.

CHAGNON, NAPOLEON A.

1977 *Yanomano: The Fierce People.* 2nd ed. New York: Holt, Rinehart & Winston.

1983 *Yanomamo: The Fierce People.* 3rd ed. New York: Holt, Rinehart & Winston.

CLENDINNEN, INGA

1980 "Landscape and World View: The Survival of Yucatec Maya Culture under Spanish Conquest." *Journal of Comparative Studies in Society and History,* 22 (1980), July: 374–395.

CLENDINNEN, INGA

1982 "Disciplining the Indians: Franciscan Ideology and Missionary Violence in Sixteenth Century Yucatan." *Past and Present.* 94: 27–48.

1987   *Ambivalent Conquests: Maya and Spaniard in Yucatan* 1517–1570. Cambridge: Cambridge University Press.

COE, MICHAEL D.
1980   *The Maya.* London: Thames & Hudson.

CRAINE, EUGENE R.
1979   *The Codex Perez and the Book of Chilam Balam of Mani.* Norman: University of Oklahoma Press.

DAVIS, VIRGINIA DALE
1978   *Ritual of the Northern Lacandon Maya.* Unpublished Ph.D. dissertation. New Orleans: Tulane University.

DE CORDOBA, FRANCISCO HERNANDEZ
1942   *The Discoverty of Yucatan.* Henry B. Wagner, transl. Berkeley: The Cortes Society.

DUBY, GERTRUDE
1944   *Los Lacandones su Pasado Y su Presente.* Mexico City: Biblioteca Enciclopedia Popular.

GEERTZ, CLIFFORD
1963   *Agricultural Involution: The Process of Ecological Change in Indonesia.* Berkeley: University of California Press.

HARRIS, ALEX, AND MARGARET SARTOR, EDS.
1984   *Gertrude Blom Bearing Witness.* Chapel Hill: University of North Carolina Press.

LOVE, BRUCE
1984   "A Yucatec Maya Agricultural Ceremony." *Estudios de Cultura Maya* 15:251–300.

MCGEE, R. JON
1983   *Sacrifice and Cannibalism: An Analysis of Myth and Ritual Among the Lacandon Maya of Chiapas Mexico.* Unpublished Ph.D. dissertation. Houston, Texas: Rice University.
1984   "The Influence of Pre-Hispanic Maya Religion in Contemporary Lacandon Ritual." *Journal of Latin American Lore,* 10(2):175–187.
1986   "Swidden Horticulture Among the Lacandon Maya." ¾ in. color video, 29 minutes, Mayan with English subtitles. Berkeley: University of California Extension Media Center.
1987   "Metaphorical Substitution in a Lacandon Maya Ritual Song." *Anthropological Linguistics,* 29(1):105–118.
1988   "Ritual Use of Balché Among the Lacandon Maya." *Estudios De Cultura Maya,* vol. XVIII, Fall 1988.
1988   "Lacandon Maya Balché Ritual" color ¾ in. video, 40 minutes, Mayan with English subtitles. Berkeley: University of California Extension Media Center.

MACKIE, SEDLEY J. (ED.)
1969   *An Account of the Conquest of Guatemala in 1524 by Pedro de Alvarado.* New York: Kraus Reprint Co.

MALER, TEOBERT

1903   *Researches in the Central Portion of the Usumacinta Valley.* Memoirs of the Peabody Museum of American Archaeology and Ethnology, vol. 2, no. 2. Cambridge: Harvard University Press.

MORLEY, SLYVANUS

1977   *The Ancient Maya.* Stanford: Stanford University Press.

NATIONS, JAMES D.

1979   *Population Ecology of the Lacandon Maya.* Unpublished Ph.D dissertation. Dallas, Tex.: Southern Methodist University.

1981   "The Rainforest Farmers." *Pacific Discovery* 24(1):1–9.

NATIONS, JAMES D., AND RONALD B. NIGH

1980   "The Evolutionary Potential of Lacandon Maya Sustained-yield Tropical Forest Agriculture." *Journal of Anthropological Research* 36(1):1–30.

NIGH, RONALD B., AND JAMES D. NATIONS

1980   "Tropical Rainforests." *The Bulletin* March:12–19.

ONG, WALTER J.

1982   *Orality and Literacy: The Technologizing of the Word.* New York: Methuen.

ORTNER, SHERRY B.

1973   "On Key Symbols." *American Anthropologist* 75:1338–1346.

PERERA, VICTOR

1988   "Signs of Renewal." *Mother Jones* February–March:36–44.

RECINOS, ADRIÁN

1978   *Popol Vuh: The Sacred Book of the Ancient Quiché Maya.* Norman: University of Oklahoma Press.

REDFIELD, ROBERT

1962   *A Village That Chose Progress: Chan Kom Revisited.* Chicago: University of Chicago Press.

1976   *Chan Kom, A Maya Village.* Chicago: University of Chicago Press.

REES, MICHAEL J.

1978   *Mathematical Models of Lacandon Maya Kinship.* Unpublished Ph.D. dissertation. New Orleans: Tulane University.

ROBICSEK, FRANCIS, AND DONALD M. HALES

1984   "Maya Heart Sacrifice: Cultural Perspective and Surgical Technique." In *Ritual Human Sacrifice in Mesoamerica.* Elizabeth H. Boone, ed. Washington, D.C.: Dumbarton Oaks.

ROYS, RALPH L.

1931   "The Ethnobotany of the Maya." *Middle American Research Series,* 2. New Orleans: Tulane University.

1967   *The Book of Chilam Balam of Chumayel.* Norman: University of Oklahoma Press.

SAPPER, KARL

1897   *Das Nordliche Mihel-Merika nelost einem ausflug nach dem Hochland von Anahuac.* Braunschweig: Friedrich Viewig und Sohn.

SCHELE, LINDA

1984   "Human Sacrifice Among the Classic Maya." In *Ritual Human Sacrifice in Mesoamerica.* Elizabeth H. Boone, ed. Washington, D.C.: Dumbarton Oaks.

SCHELE, LINDA, AND MARY ELLEN MILLER

1986   *The Blood of Kings, Dynasty and Ritual in Maya Art.* New York: George Braziller.

SCHOLES, FRANCE V., AND RALPH L. ROYS

1938   "Fray Diego de Landa and the Problem of Idolatry in Yucatan." *Cooperation in Research.* Publication 501. Carnegie Institution of Washington.

1968   *The Maya Chontal Indians of Acalan—Tixchel.* Norman: University of Oklahoma Press.

SOUSTELLE, JACQUES

1984   "Ritual Human Sacrifice in Mesoamerica: An Introduction." In *Ritual Human Sacrifice in Mesoamerica.* Elizabeth H. Boone, ed. Washington, D.C.: Dumbarton Oaks.

STEPHENS, JOHN L.

1969   *Incidents of Travel in Central America, Chiapas, and Yucatan.* New York: Dover.

TEDLOCK, BARBARA

1985   *Time and the Highland Maya.* Albuquerque: University of New Mexico Press.

THOMPSON, J. E. S.

1952   "Waxen Idols and a Sacrificial Rite of the Lacandones." *Carnegie Institution of Washington Notes on Middle American Anthropology and Ethnology.* 4(109): 193–195.

1954   *The Rise and Fall of Maya Civilization.* 1st ed. Norman: University of Oklahoma Press.

1966   *The Rise and Fall of Maya Civilization.* 2nd ed. Norman: University of Oklahoma Press.

1972   *Maya History and Religion.* Norman: University of Oklahoma Press.

TOZZER, ALFRED MARSTON

1902–1905 *Archaeological Institute of America/American Journal of Archaeology, second series, Journal of the Archaeological Institute of America,* vol. 6 supplement:2–4; vol 7 supplement: 45–47; vol. 8 supplement: 54–56; vol. 9 supplement: 41–47.

1907   *A Comparative Study of the Mayas and the Lacandones.* New York: Macmillan.

1913 "A Spanish Manuscript Letter." *18th International Congress of the Americas* 2:497–509. London.

1978 *Landa's Relacion de Las Cosas de Yucatan.* Millwood, N.Y.: Krause.

VILLACORTA, J. ANTONIO C., AND CARLOS A. VILLACORTA

1933 *Codices Mayas: Dresden Peresianus, Trocortesianus.* Guatemala, C.A.: Tipografia Nacional.

VOGT, EVON Z.

1969 *Zinacantan: A Maya Community in the Highlands of Chiapas.* Cambridge, Mass.: Harvard University Press.

1970 *The Zinacantecos of Mexico: A Modern Maya Way of Life.* New York: Holt, Rinehart & Winston.

WAGNER, HENRY R.

1942 *The Discovery of Yucatan by Francisco Hernandez de Cordoba.* Berkeley: The Cortes Society.

WALLACE, A. F. C.

1966 *Religion: An Anthropological View.* New York: Random House.

WILKERSON, S. JEFFREY K.

1984 "In Search of the Mountain of Foam: Human Sacrifice in Eastern Mesoamerica." In *Ritual Human Sacrifice in Mesoamerica.* Elizabeth H. Boone, ed: Washington, D.C.: Dumbarton Oaks.

Glossary: Selected Lacandon, Spanish, and Anthropological Terms

Aak'ä Lacandon for *darkness.*

Acahuale A swidden garden that has been left fallow.

Affinal kin Individuals related by marriage.

Ahau Prehispanic Mayan official title meaning *lord.*

Äk'inchob Lacandon god of the milpa.

Äkyantho' The Lacandon god of foreigners and foreign objects.

Äkyum *Our Lord;* another term for the Lacandons' principal deity Hachäkyum.

Annatto Lacandon *k'uxu,* a red vegetable dye made from the plant *Bixa orellana* and used as symbolic blood in Lacandon rituals.

Atole A cooked corn gruel.

Ayim Lacandon for alligator.

Baak The Lacandon word for *bone* or *plastic.*

Ba'ats The Lacandon term for *howler monkey.*

Bäk nikte The *Plumeria rubra* flower; sacred to the Lacandons because they believe the gods were born from it.

Balché A mildly intoxicating mead, brewed specifically for Mayan religious ceremonies, using honey and the bark of the balché tree *(Lonchocarpus longistylus).* The Lacandon believe drinking this beverage makes a person spiritually and physically pure.

Balché chem The mahogany dugout canoe in which the Lacandon ferment balché.

Balum Lacandon for *jaguar.*

Bol The Lacandon god of balché.

Bonampak Classic Period Mayan ruins near the Lacandon village of Lacanha Chan Sayab. Rooms at Bonampak contain murals depicting Mayan royalty.

Breadnut Lacandon *ox,* a tree *(Brosium alicastrum)* with edible fruit and seeds.

Bride service When a young man works for his wife's father in payment for his new bride. Young Lacandon men's bride service is for a period of time that is negotiated with his future father-in-law during courtship, usually for one or two years.

Bulha'kilutalk'in Another name for the god *Chäk Ik Al,* the deity associated with hurricanes, the color red, and the direction east.

Ceiba A tropical rainforest tree sacred to the Maya. These trees are believed to stand at the four corners and the center of the earth, holding the layers of the cosmos apart.

Cenote A natural limestone well. The word is derived from the Maya word *tzonot.*

Chacs The Prehispanic Mayan gods of rain; associated with the colors red, black, yellow, and white and the four cardinal directions.

Chäk hu'un Headbands dyed red and worn in Lacandon rituals; made from the bark of the amate tree *(Ficus* sp.).

Chamula Tzotzil-speaking Mayan Indians who live in the municipio of San Juan Chamula, Chiapas.

Chan A Lacandon word meaning *little;* often used as a prefix in names such as Chan K'in, or "Little K'in."

Chayote *Also* Lacandon *p'ish;* a pear-shaped vegetable *(Sechium edule)* that tastes something like a potato; grown in Lacandon milpas.

Che' Lacandon for *wood.*

Chem A Lacandon dugout canoe; also the vessel in which balché is brewed.

Chembel K'uh The "minor gods," servants to the principal pantheon of Lacandon gods.

Chicle The sap of a tree used in the manufacture of chewing gum.

Chicleros Those who tap the sap of the chicle tree.

Chiich Lacandon for *maternal grandmother.*

Ch'ik'ink'uh "The god who eats the sun"; the direction west.

Chilam Balam of Chumayel A Prehispanic Yucatecan Maya book of history and prophecy.

Chixokla The Lacandon name for the ruins of Yaxchilan.

Chol A dialect of the Mayan language. The term also identifies speakers of this language.

Chul ha' *Sacred water;* a ritual name for atole.

Chun lucht-ik "To give the base" of a drinking gourd; that is, to compel a person to drink balché until they vomit. Individuals undergo the chun lucht-ik as punishment for minor transgressions.

Compadre *Godfather.* A man who accepts the role of compadre agrees to aid the parents of his godchild as well as to become this child's guardian. In Latin America, people create systems of political and financial support both by requesting individuals accept godparentage of their children and by sponsoring these children on important ritual occasions such as baptisms, confirmations, and weddings.

Consanguineal kin "Blood" kin. Individuals related by birth.

Copal Pine resin incense tapped from the Copal tree *(Protium copal).*

Dresden Codex One of three Prehispanic Maya hieroglyphic books to survive the Spaniard's conquest of the Maya.

Entrada An armed reconnaissance into unknown territory; the Spaniards conducted many entradas through Chiapas and Guatemala looking for hostile Mayan communities.

H-men Yucatecan Maya shaman; *see also To'ohil.*

Ha'an Lacandon for *son-in-law.*

Haawo' The raccoon onen.

Hach Lacandon word meaning *real* or *true;* for example, *hach t'an,* "real language."

Ha'hanak'uh The assistants of Mensäbäk, the Lacandon god of rain.

Hesuklistos Lacandon for "Jesus Christ."

Hetzmek A Yucatecan Maya birth ritual in which a newborn baby is introduced to the tools and objects it will use as an adult.

Hiloletik Zinacantecan Maya shaman; *See also To'ohil.*

Ho'ol The Lacandon term for *head;* the term can also refer to the top of something, such as *ho'ol nah che,* "the top roof beam of a house"; or the first or primary object, for example, the *ts'aik u ho'ol* ceremony, which is a ritual offering of the first foods harvested from a milpa.

Horticulture Simple garden agriculture in which only hand tools such as machetes and digging sticks are utilized.

Huipil The traditional Yucatecan Maya woman's skirt or smock.

Huncame One of the heroic characters in the Popol Vuh, a mythic chronology of the Quiche Maya.

Hunhunahpu Brother of Huncame; another of the heroic characters in the Popol Vuh, a mythic chronology of the Quiche Maya.

Hunk²uk² Lacandon for *eagle.*

Hu²un Lacandon for *paper* or *book; chäk hu²un* are bark cloth headbands dyed red and worn during Lacandon rituals.

Huyu² Minature wooden spoon used to feed the god pots.

Itza A migratory Mayan people who settled in the Yucatán peninsula during the thirteenth century and gave their name to the Toltec Mayan site of Chichen Itza.

Itzamna "Alligator Lord"; Prehispanic Yucatecan Maya creator deity.

Itsanok²uh "Great Alligator God"; Lacandon deity whose name is derived from Itzamna, *see* Table 6.1.

Ixchel Daughter of Hachäkyum and the Lacandon goddess of childbirth.

Ka²an Lacandon for *sky* or *heaven.*

Kah A derogatory name the Lacandon use for non–Lacandon Indians. For example, the Lacandon call Tzeltal Maya "kah."

K²ak² *Fire;* the Lacandon god of war and disease.

Käkäoh *Cacao,* a chocolate beverage like cocoa.

K²akoch The supreme Lacandon deity, the creator of the gods and the universe.

Kanche Low stools on which Lacandon men sit during rituals in the god house.

Katun The *tun* was the 360 day "year" in the Prehispanic Mayan calendar; a katun is 20 tuns, or 7,200 days.

K²ayum The Lacandon god of song; *see* Table 6.1.

Kib Any small light such as a candle or flashlight. Candles are left as funerary offerings on Lacandon graves and symbolize death in Lacandon dream symbolism.

Kinyah A Lacandon divination ceremony.

K²ik² Minature humanoid figures made from natural latex rubber that are burned as offerings in Lacandon incense burners; also the root of the word for *blood.*

K²in The Lacandon word for *sun;* also a common name for Lacandon men.

Kisin The Lacandon god of death.

Kitam *Javelina,* a white-lipped peccary; hunted by Lacandon men.

Kol The Lacandon term for their rainforest gardens; *See also milpa.*

K²uh The Lacandon word for *god.*

K²uxu *Annatto (Bixa orellana),* a red vegetable dye used as symbolic blood in Lacandon rituals.

K²uk²ulkan/Quetzalcoatl "Feathered Serpent." To the Prehispanic Maya and peoples of Central Mexico, *K²uk²ulcan/Quetzalcoatl* was an extremely important figure in both religious and mythic histories. A mythic hero credited with settling the site of Tula, according to Coe (1980); he may also have been a historical person who led a Toltec migration into the Yucatán Peninsula, settling at Chichen Itza in the latter half of the tenth century. By the time of the conquest, *K²uk²ulkan/Quetzalcoatl* had become a mythic hero figure throughout Mesoamerica. In contemporary Lacandon belief, *K²uk²ulkan* is one of Hachäkyum's pets, a malevolent giant serpent who will help destroy humans at the end of the present creation. See Carasco (1984) for a discussion of variations on the *K²uk²ulkan/Quetzalcoatl* mythic theme.

K²ulel An assistant to Hachäkyum.

Lacanha The name of a southern Lacandon Maya community.

Lak The Lacandon term for *spouse*.

Läkil K'uh *God pot,* a Lacandon incense burner.

Luuch Balché drinking gourds or a cup.

Ma'ats Ground corn dough mixed with water to form an uncooked corn gruel. Men carry small balls of corn dough with them when they travel or go hunting, and mix the dough with water to make a quick meal.

Manioc In Lacandon, *tz'in;* a tropical rainforest root crop *(Manihot esculenta).*

Manos Hand-held stones used with a metate to grind vegetable foods.

Matrilocal The practice in which a newly married couple lives with the bride's family.

Me'et Wicker rings used as coasters for gourds full of balché. The *me'et* hold the gourds upright, keeping them from touching the ground and polluting the balché.

Mek'chul The Lacandon rite that initiates adolescent men and women into adulthood. One cannot marry or conduct rituals in the god house until after the *mek'chul* ceremony. Parents also use this ritual as an opportunity to make a major payment of food and balché offerings to the gods, thanking the gods for allowing their children to survive.

Mensäbäk "Maker of Powder," the Lacandon god of rain.

Metate The stone platform upon which vegetable materials are ground with a mano.

Metla'an The Lacandon underworld where spirits of the dead must undergo a series of trials; also called *Yalam Lu'um.*

Milpa The Spanish term for a tropical rainforest garden; *see also Kol.*

Nagual Similar to a European witch's animal familiar, *naguals* are the animals that witches transform themselves into in Latin American belief.

Nah tsulu Giant celestial jaguars, pets of Hachäkyum who will help destroy humans at the end of the present creation.

Nahwah Ceremonial tamales filled with either beans or meat; used as symbolic substitutes for human flesh.

Nahwahto' An ancient people in Lacandon mythology who were said to be cannibals. In Lacandon mythology, the *Nahwahto'* are described as cutting the hearts out of their captives, feeding the heart and blood to their god pots, and then consuming the victim's body. Given that these actions are a description of actual treatment given to Mayan captives taken in battle, it is likely that the *Nahwahto'* were a historical people.

Na'il The Lacandon term for *the wife of.* For example, Xkale'ox, Hachäkyum's wife, is called *U Na'il Hachäkyum.*

Nukuch winik The "Ancient One," the ancestral hero figure in most Lacandon myths. He is said to have traveled to the underworld and been the lover of Kisin's (the god of death) daughter. Also called Lehikähbäh, the "Trapper of Moles."

Onen An animal name and kin affiliation inherited from one's father. For example, Chan K'in Viejo's "official" name is Chan K'in Ma'ax, or "Chan K'in Spider Monkey." Ma'ax is his onen. At one time, the Lacandon may have chosen spouses from within their onens, but this practice no longer exists.

Paho The guatapil palm. Its fruit is edible and its leaves used for roofing material.

Pak A large clay pot that Lacandon men use to carry balché from the balché chem to the god house. Once in the god house, balché is ladled from this container into individual drinking gourds.

Palenque Classic Period Maya ruins sacred to the Lacandon.

Pätak che During rituals, the Lacandon take their god pots down from storage on a shelf in the rafters of the god house and place the incense burners on rows of mahogany boards facing the east. *Pätak che* is the name for these boards.

Patrilocal The practice in which a newly married couple resides with the husband's family.

Pixan *Spirit, soul,* or *ghost.* The spiritual entity that continues to exist after death. Also refers to one's heartbeat, pulse, or respiration.

Polygyny A form of polygamy; having more than one wife. Some Lacandon men are polygynous.

Pom Copal (pine resin) incense.

Popol Vuh Prehispanic mythic history of the Quiche Maya.

Puuna The mahogany tree. The Lacandon use mahogany for making furniture and dugout canoes.

Quiche Maya A Mayan people who live in the highlands of Guatemala. They were conquered in 1523 by Alvarado, one of Cortes's officers.

Säk Ha$^{?}$ *White water,* a cooked corn gruel called *atole* in Spanish.

Sapodilla The Lacandon eat the fruit of this tree *(Manilkara zapota).*

Sil Small god pots for the assistants to the major gods.

Sororal polygyny When a man has more than one wife and the women are sisters.

Suhuy k$^{?}$ak$^{?}$ *Virgin fire;* a fire kindled to light incense offerings.

Sukunkyum Older Brother of Hachäkyum, chief lord of the underworld and judge of souls after death.

Swidden horticulture Also called "slash-and-burn" horticulture, this form of gardening is marked by the cutting of brush and trees in a field; when the vegetation is dry, it is burned to fertilize the field. This form of horticulture is usually found in tropical areas today.

T$^{?}$an The Lacandon word for *word* or *speech.*

Ta$^{?}$k$^{?}$in Literally *excrement of the sun,* this is the Mayan word for gold, coins, or money.

To$^{?}$ohil A Lacandon ritual leader, believed to be supernaturally powerful.

Totem An animal, plant, object, or mythic figure believed to be the progenitor of a lineage or clan.

Tro-Cortesiano One of three Prehispanic Mayan hieroglyphic books to survive the Spaniard's conquest of the Maya.

Ts$^{?}$ibatnah "Painter of Houses", *see* Table 6.1.

Tsul The Lacandon term for light-skinned foreigners.

Tsup The *agouti,* a large rodent *(Dasyprocta mexicana)* hunted by the Lacandon for food.

Tukul The Lacandon term for *thoughtful* or *pensive.*

T$^{?}$ul Lacandon for *rabbit.*

Tunsel The *pileated woodpecker;* also a character in Lacandon mythology.

Tus Lacandon for *lie.*

T$^{?}$ut$^{?}$ Lacandon for *parrot.*

Tzeltal One dialect of the Mayan language. The term is also used to identify speakers of this language.

Tz$^{?}$in *See* Manioc.

Tzotzil A dialect of the Mayan language. The term is also used to identify speakers of this language.

Uuk Lacandon for *dove.*

Wech Lacandon for *armadillo*.

Wes The Lacandon word for an *authority, judge,* or *police officer*.

Winik The Lacandon word for *person* or *people*.

Xa'an The leaves of the unspined salt palm *(Sabal mexicana)*, which are used as ground cover for drinking gourds during the balché ritual, to cover the balché chem, and as roof-thatching material.

Xaté Leaves of the guatapil palm (*Chamaedoria* spp.) used in curing rituals and to feed the gods balché.

Xaman Lacandon for *north*.

Xibalba The Quiche Maya underworld.

Xikal A flat board shaped like a broad paddle, upon which Lacandon men symbolically arrange incense offerings that represent human beings.

Xikin Lacandon for *ear*.

Xikul The traditional, ankle-length Lacandon smock worn by both men and women.

Xka'le'ox "She of the breadnut leaf," creator of women and wife of Hachäkyum.

Xtabay A spirit of the forest who appears to young men as a beautiful woman, and seduces, then strangles them.

Ya'ahk'in A type of Lacandon ritual in which the first fruits of a field are offered to the gods.

Yalam lu'um The Lacandon underworld where spirits of the dead must undergo a series of trials; also called *Metla'an*.

Yatoch k'uh Lacandon for *god house;* the structure in which Lacandon ceremonies are conducted.

Yaxchilan Classic Period Mayan archeological site. A sacred site to the Lacandon, who believe it is the home of their gods and make pilgrimages there to present offerings to these deities.

Yuk Lacandon for *deer*.

Yum Lacandon for *Lord* or *uncle*.

Yumbili Ka'an "Lord of the Sky," one of Hachäkyum's titles.

Index